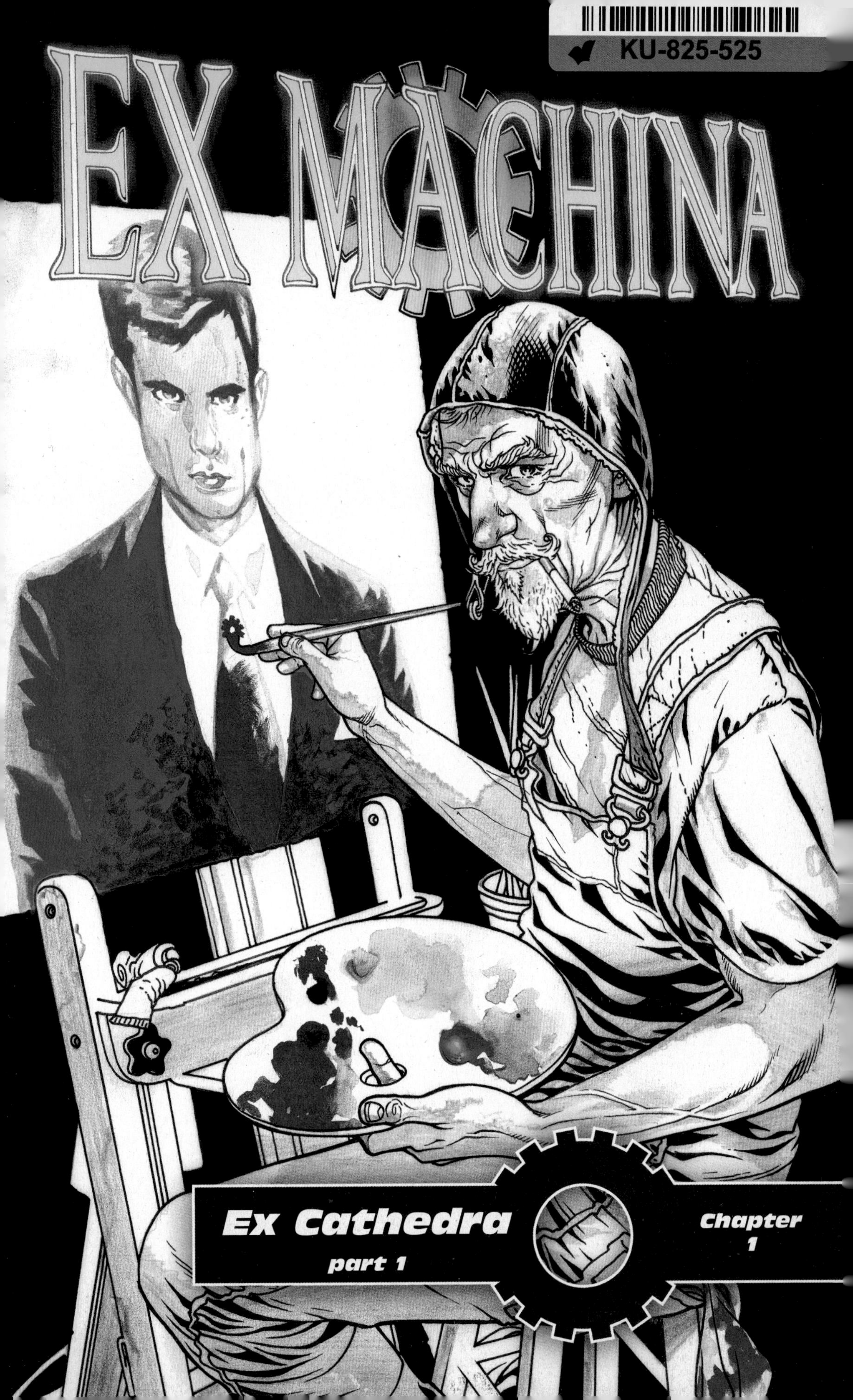
EX MACHINA
Ex Cathedra
part 1
Chapter
1

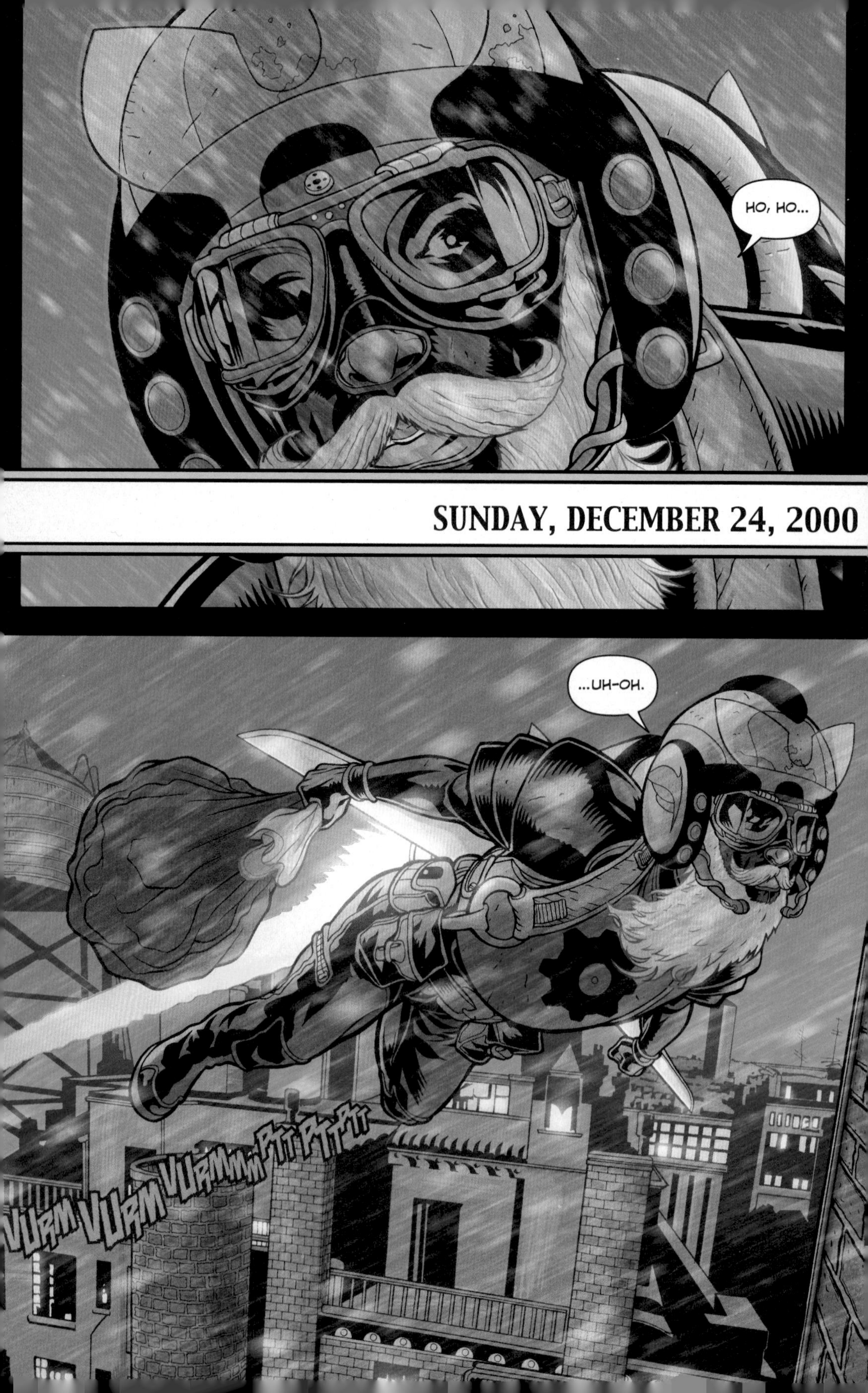
HO, HO...
SUNDAY, DECEMBER 24, 2000
...UH-OH.
VURM VURM VURMMMM PTT PTTPTT

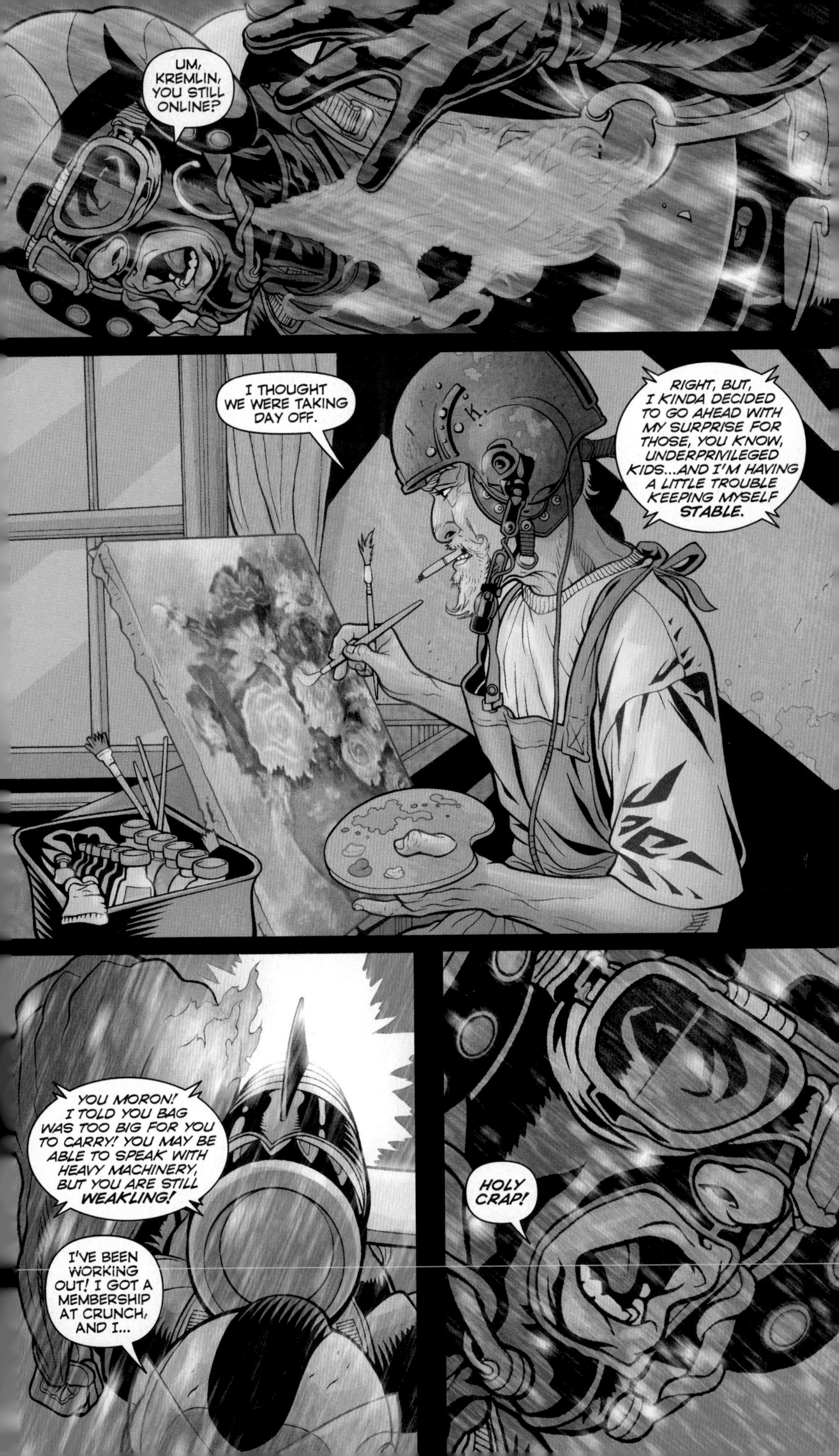
UM, KREMLIN, YOU STILL ONLINE?
I THOUGHT WE WERE TAKING DAY OFF.
RIGHT, BUT, I KINDA DECIDED TO GO AHEAD WITH MY SURPRISE FOR THOSE, YOU KNOW, UNDERPRIVILEGED KIDS...AND I'M HAVING A LITTLE TROUBLE KEEPING MYSELF STABLE.
YOU MORON! I TOLD YOU BAG WAS TOO BIG FOR YOU TO CARRY! YOU MAY BE ABLE TO SPEAK WITH HEAVY MACHINERY, BUT YOU ARE STILL WEAKLING!
I'VE BEEN WORKING OUT! I GOT A MEMBERSHIP AT CRUNCH, AND I...
HOLY CRAP!

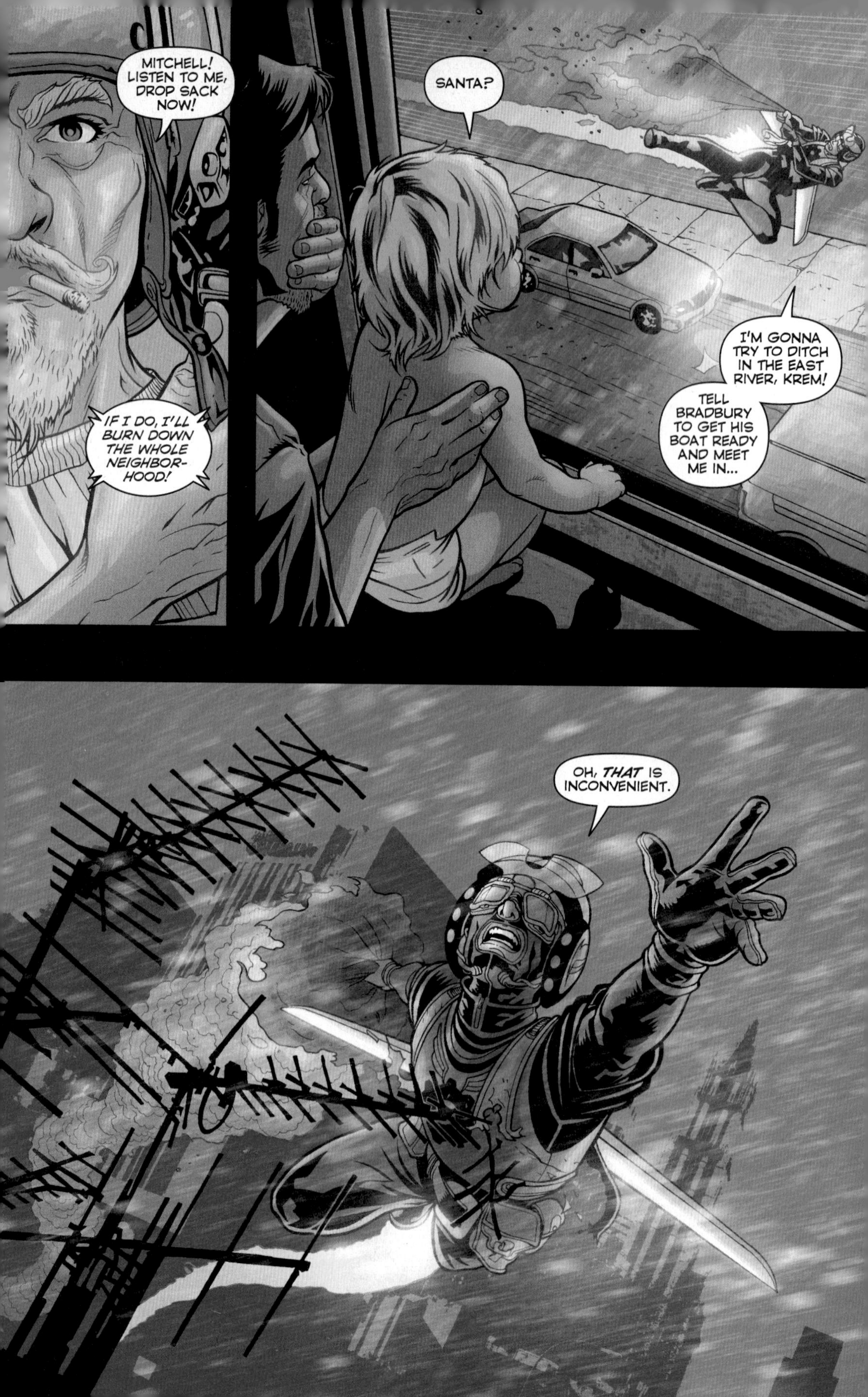
MITCHELL! LISTEN TO ME, DROP SACK NOW!
IF I DO, I'LL BURN DOWN THE WHOLE NEIGHBOR-HOOD!
SANTA?
I'M GONNA TRY TO DITCH IN THE EAST RIVER, KREM!
TELL BRADBURY TO GET HIS BOAT READY AND MEET ME IN...
OH, THAT IS INCONVENIENT.

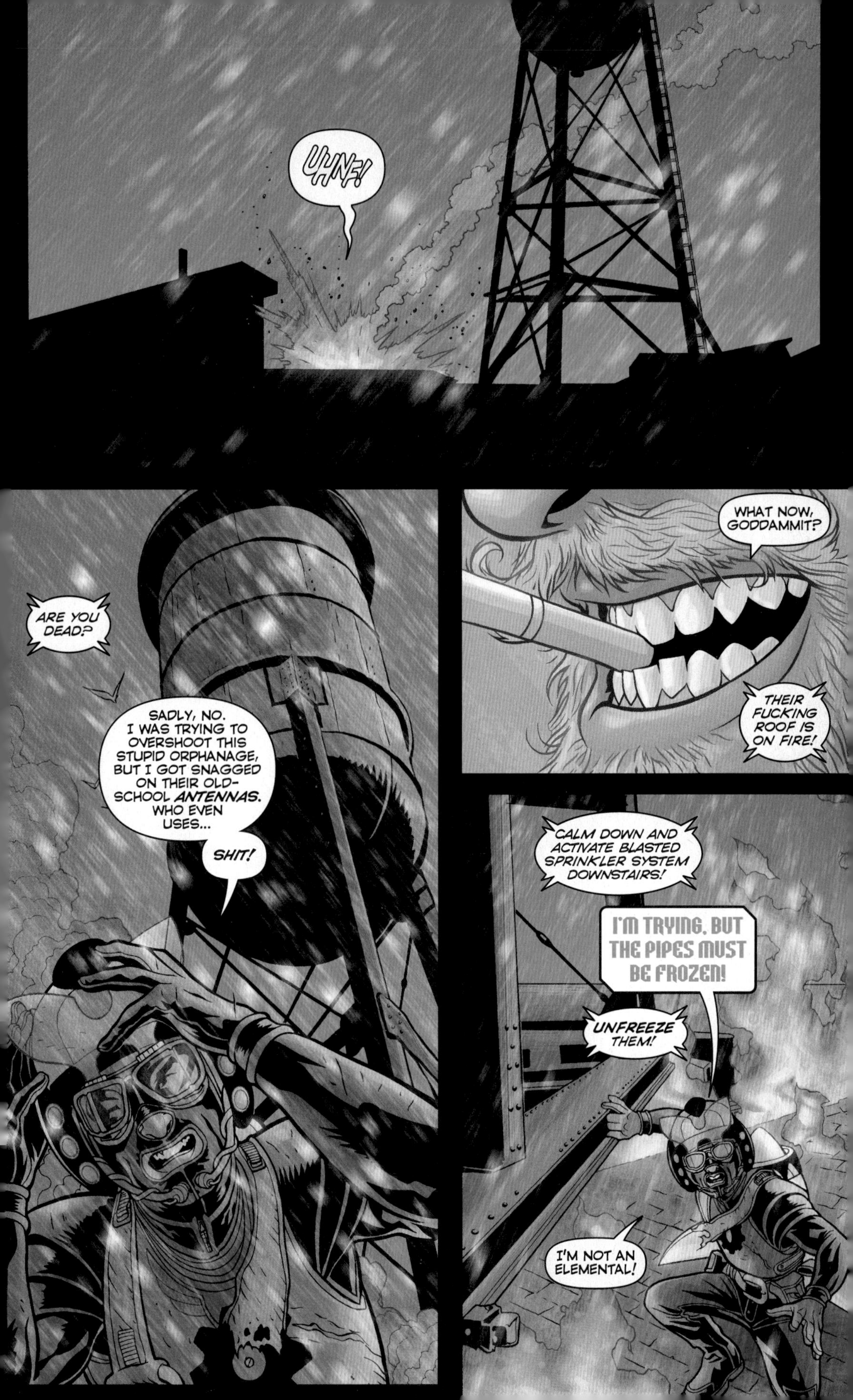
UHNF!
ARE YOU DEAD?
SADLY, NO. I WAS TRYING TO OVERSHOOT THIS STUPID ORPHANAGE, BUT I GOT SNAGGED ON THEIR OLD-SCHOOL ANTENNAS. WHO EVEN USES...
SHIT!
WHAT NOW, GODDAMMIT?
THEIR FUCKING ROOF IS ON FIRE!
CALM DOWN AND ACTIVATE BLASTED SPRINKLER SYSTEM DOWNSTAIRS!
I'M TRYING, BUT THE PIPES MUST BE FROZEN!
UNFREEZE THEM!
I'M NOT AN ELEMENTAL!

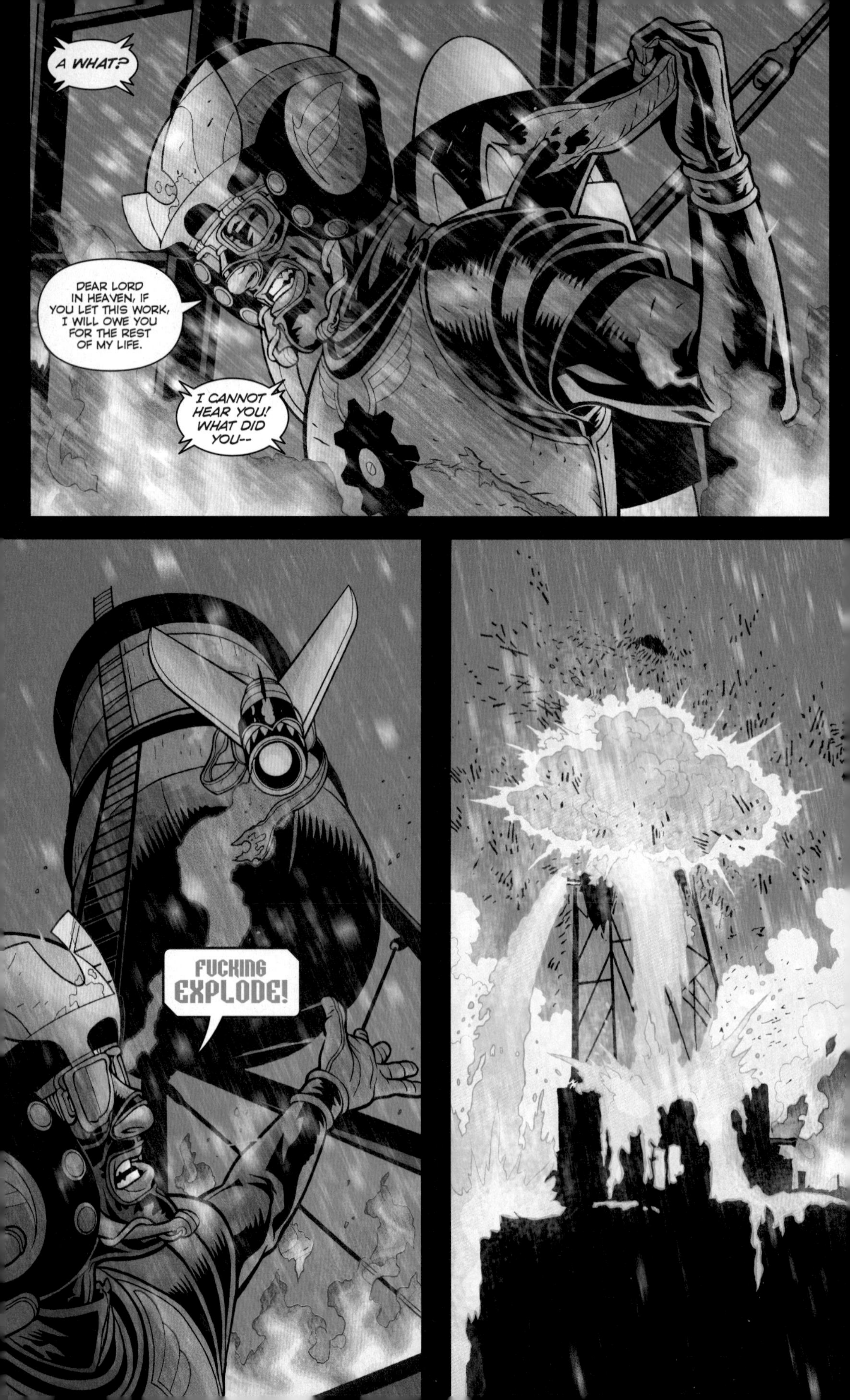
A WHAT?
DEAR LORD IN HEAVEN, IF YOU LET THIS WORK, I WILL OWE YOU FOR THE REST OF MY LIFE.
I CANNOT HEAR YOU! WHAT DID YOU--
FUCKING EXPLODE!

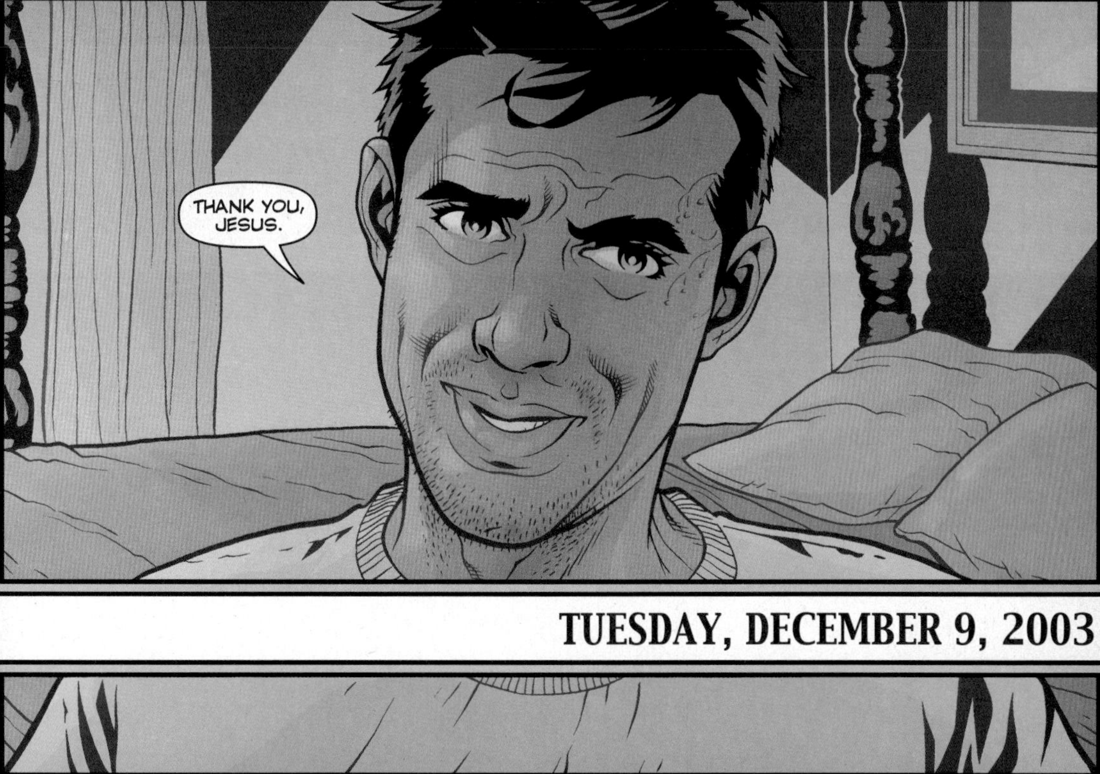
THANK YOU, JESUS.
TUESDAY, DECEMBER 9, 2003

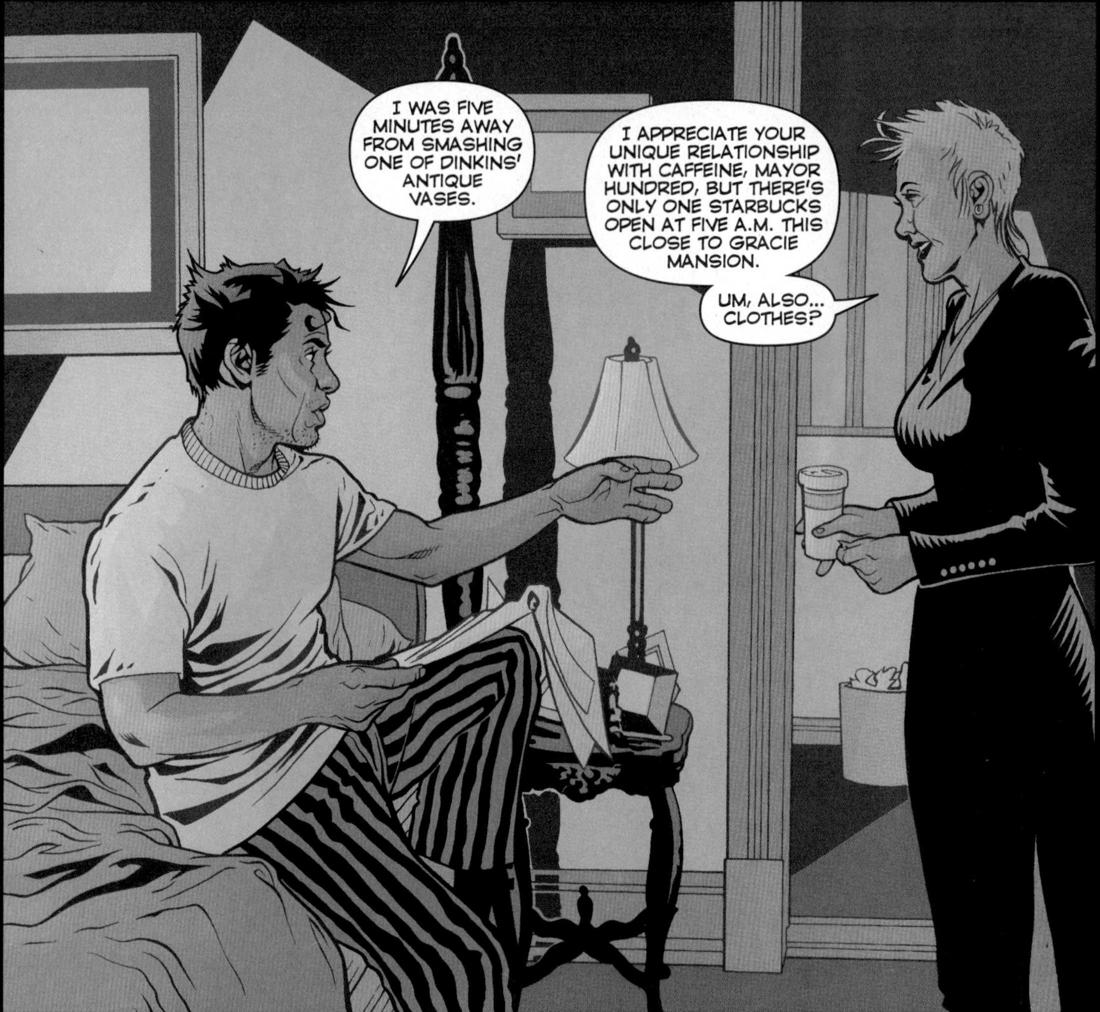
I WAS FIVE MINUTES AWAY FROM SMASHING ONE OF DINKINS' ANTIQUE VASES.
I APPRECIATE YOUR UNIQUE RELATIONSHIP WITH CAFFEINE, MAYOR HUNDRED, BUT THERE'S ONLY ONE STARBUCKS OPEN AT FIVE A.M. THIS CLOSE TO GRACIE MANSION.
UM, ALSO... CLOTHES?

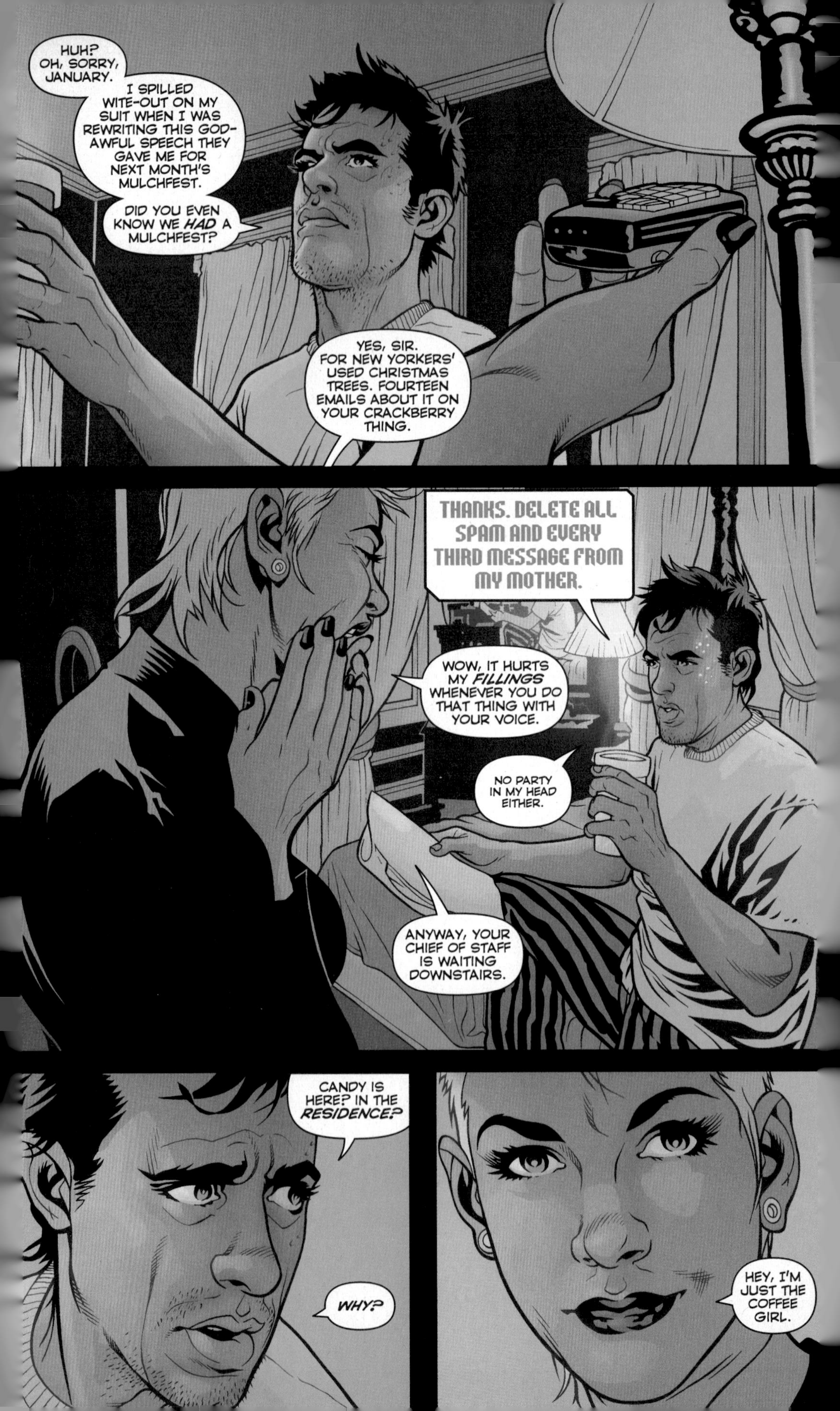
HUH? OH, SORRY, JANUARY.
I SPILLED WITE-OUT ON MY SUIT WHEN I WAS REWRITING THIS GOD-AWFUL SPEECH THEY GAVE ME FOR NEXT MONTH'S MULCHFEST.
DID YOU EVEN KNOW WE *HAD* A MULCHFEST?
YES, SIR. FOR NEW YORKERS' USED CHRISTMAS TREES. FOURTEEN EMAILS ABOUT IT ON YOUR CRACKBERRY THING.
THANKS. DELETE ALL SPAM AND EVERY THIRD MESSAGE FROM MY MOTHER.
WOW, IT HURTS MY *FILLINGS* WHENEVER YOU DO THAT THING WITH YOUR VOICE.
NO PARTY IN MY HEAD EITHER.
ANYWAY, YOUR CHIEF OF STAFF IS WAITING DOWNSTAIRS.
CANDY IS HERE? IN THE *RESIDENCE?*
WHY?
HEY, I'M JUST THE COFFEE GIRL.

The Zombie Pirate Padeem

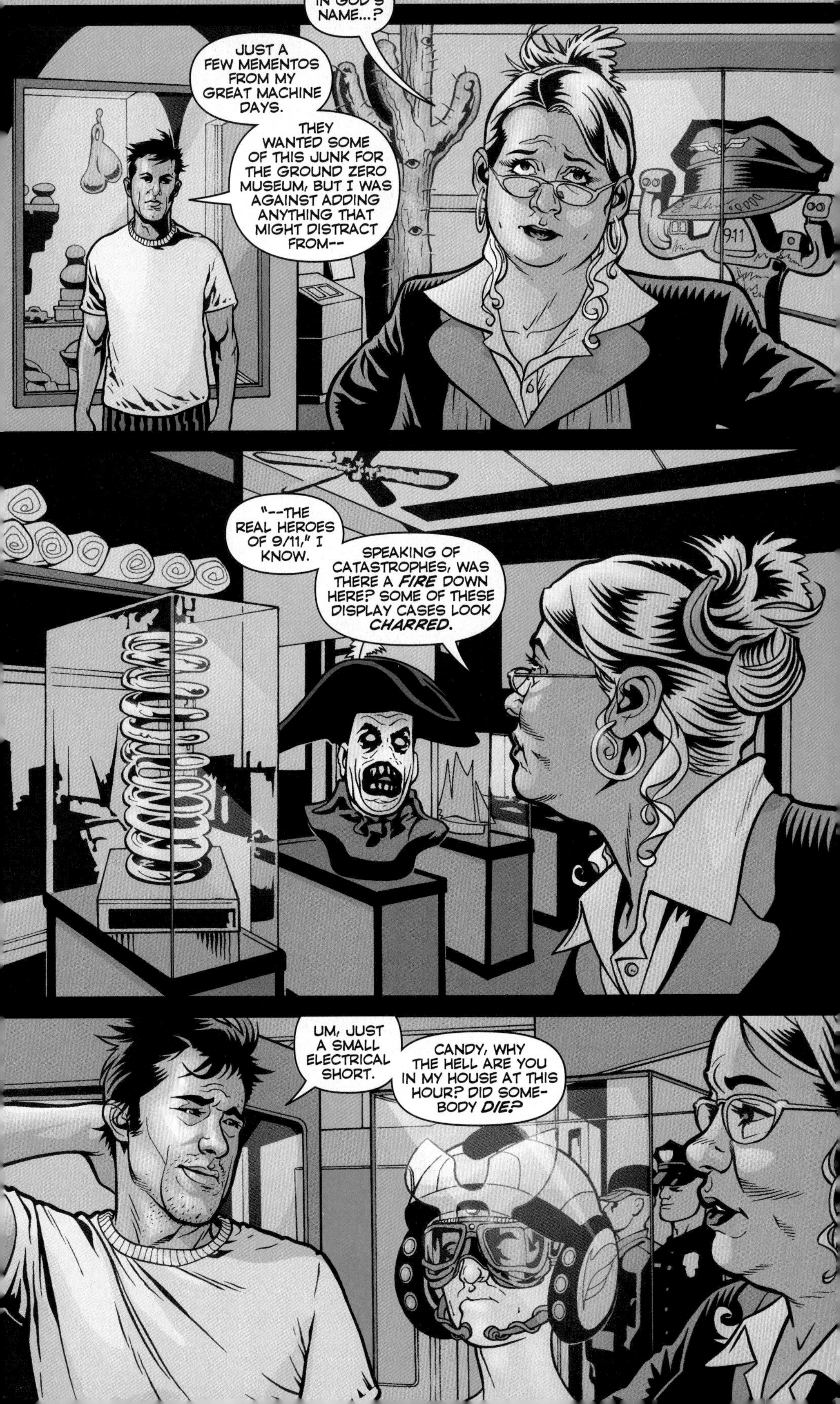
WHAT IN GOD'S NAME...?
JUST A FEW MEMENTOS FROM MY GREAT MACHINE DAYS.
THEY WANTED SOME OF THIS JUNK FOR THE GROUND ZERO MUSEUM, BUT I WAS AGAINST ADDING ANYTHING THAT MIGHT DISTRACT FROM--
9-11
"--THE REAL HEROES OF 9/11," I KNOW.
SPEAKING OF CATASTROPHES, WAS THERE A *FIRE* DOWN HERE? SOME OF THESE DISPLAY CASES LOOK **CHARRED**.
UM, JUST A SMALL ELECTRICAL SHORT.
CANDY, WHY THE HELL ARE YOU IN MY HOUSE AT THIS HOUR? DID SOMEBODY *DIE?*

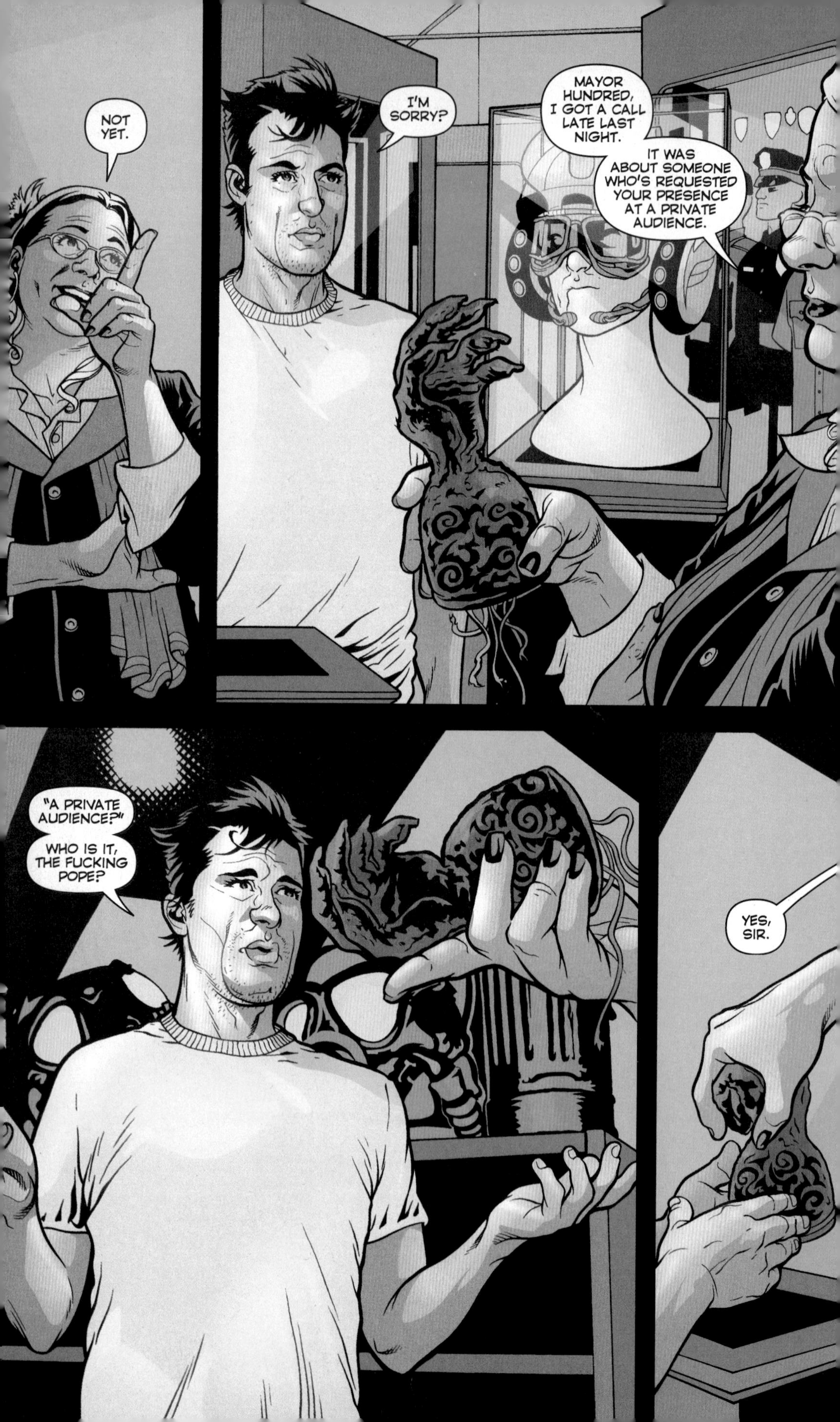
NOT YET.
I'M SORRY?
MAYOR HUNDRED, I GOT A CALL LATE LAST NIGHT.
IT WAS ABOUT SOMEONE WHO'S REQUESTED YOUR PRESENCE AT A PRIVATE AUDIENCE.
"A PRIVATE AUDIENCE?"
WHO IS IT, THE FUCKING POPE?
YES, SIR.

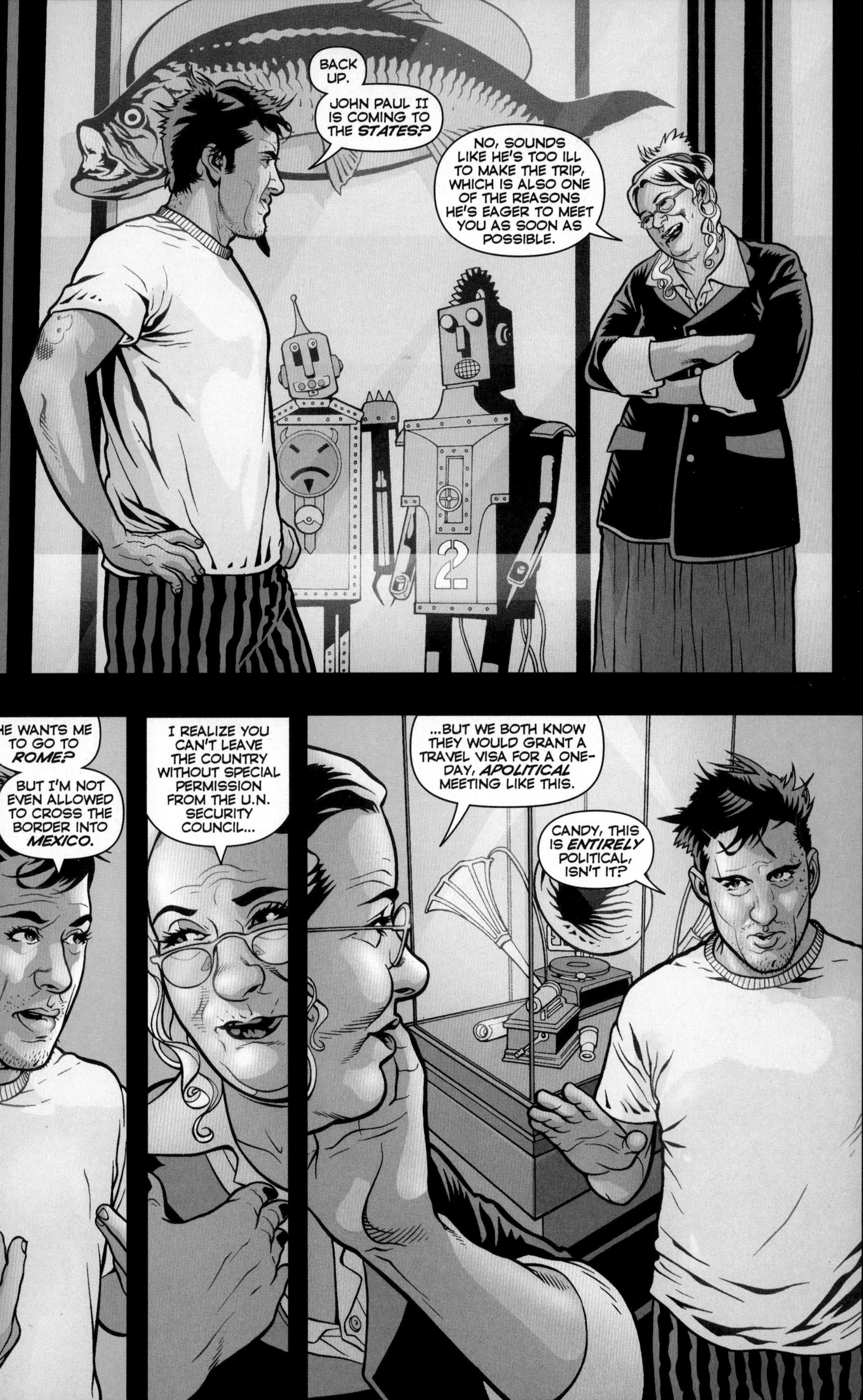
BACK UP.
JOHN PAUL II IS COMING TO THE STATES?
NO, SOUNDS LIKE HE'S TOO ILL TO MAKE THE TRIP, WHICH IS ALSO ONE OF THE REASONS HE'S EAGER TO MEET YOU AS SOON AS POSSIBLE.
HE WANTS ME TO GO TO ROME?
BUT I'M NOT EVEN ALLOWED TO CROSS THE BORDER INTO MEXICO.
I REALIZE YOU CAN'T LEAVE THE COUNTRY WITHOUT SPECIAL PERMISSION FROM THE U.N. SECURITY COUNCIL...
...BUT WE BOTH KNOW THEY WOULD GRANT A TRAVEL VISA FOR A ONE-DAY, APOLITICAL MEETING LIKE THIS.
CANDY, THIS IS ENTIRELY POLITICAL, ISN'T IT?
2

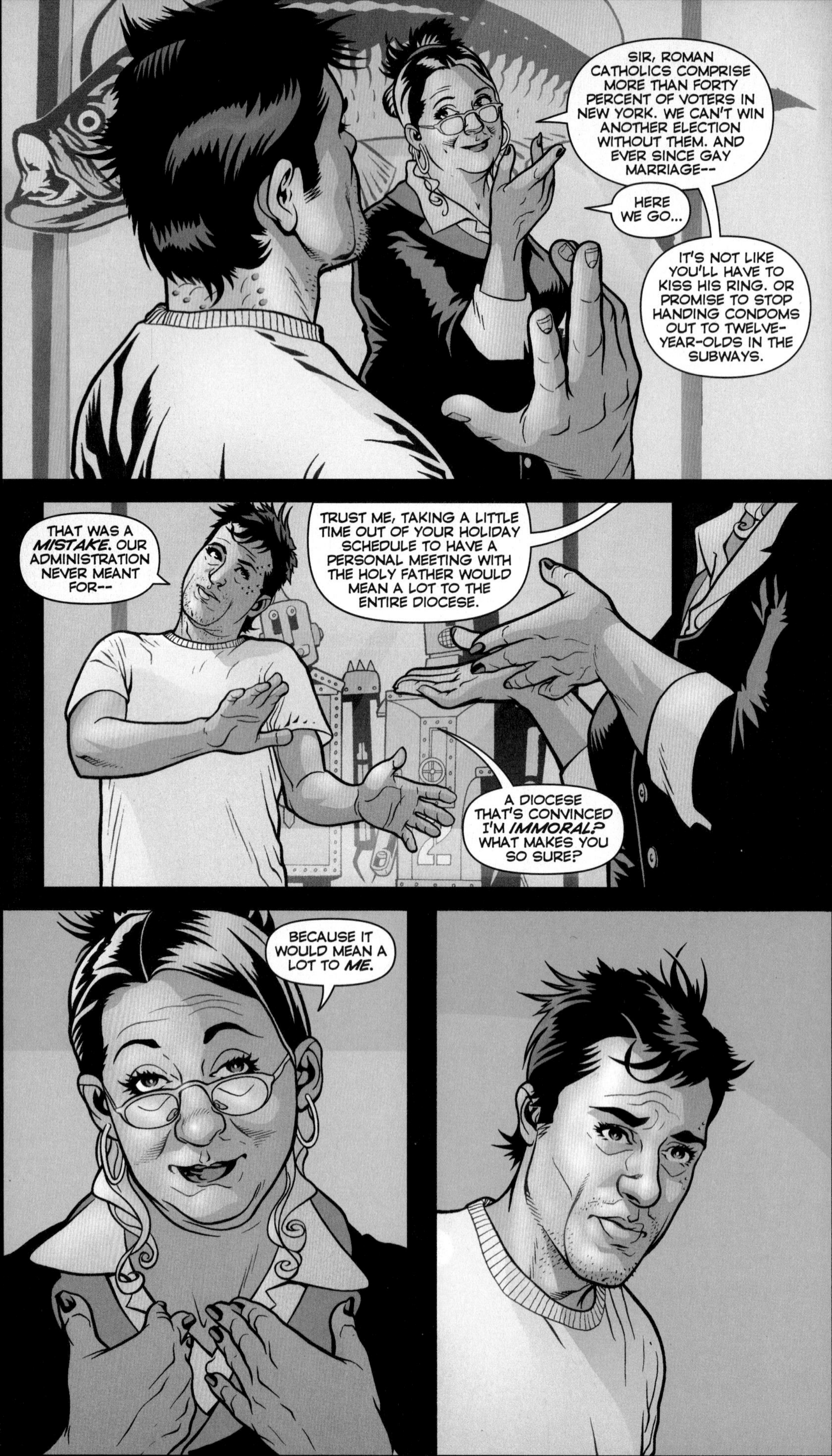
SIR, ROMAN CATHOLICS COMPRISE MORE THAN FORTY PERCENT OF VOTERS IN NEW YORK. WE CAN'T WIN ANOTHER ELECTION WITHOUT THEM. AND EVER SINCE GAY MARRIAGE--
HERE WE GO...
IT'S NOT LIKE YOU'LL HAVE TO KISS HIS RING. OR PROMISE TO STOP HANDING CONDOMS OUT TO TWELVE-YEAR-OLDS IN THE SUBWAYS.
THAT WAS A *MISTAKE*. OUR ADMINISTRATION NEVER MEANT FOR--
TRUST ME, TAKING A LITTLE TIME OUT OF YOUR HOLIDAY SCHEDULE TO HAVE A PERSONAL MEETING WITH THE HOLY FATHER WOULD MEAN A LOT TO THE ENTIRE DIOCESE.
A DIOCESE THAT'S CONVINCED I'M *IMMORAL?* WHAT MAKES YOU SO SURE?
BECAUSE IT WOULD MEAN A LOT TO *ME*.

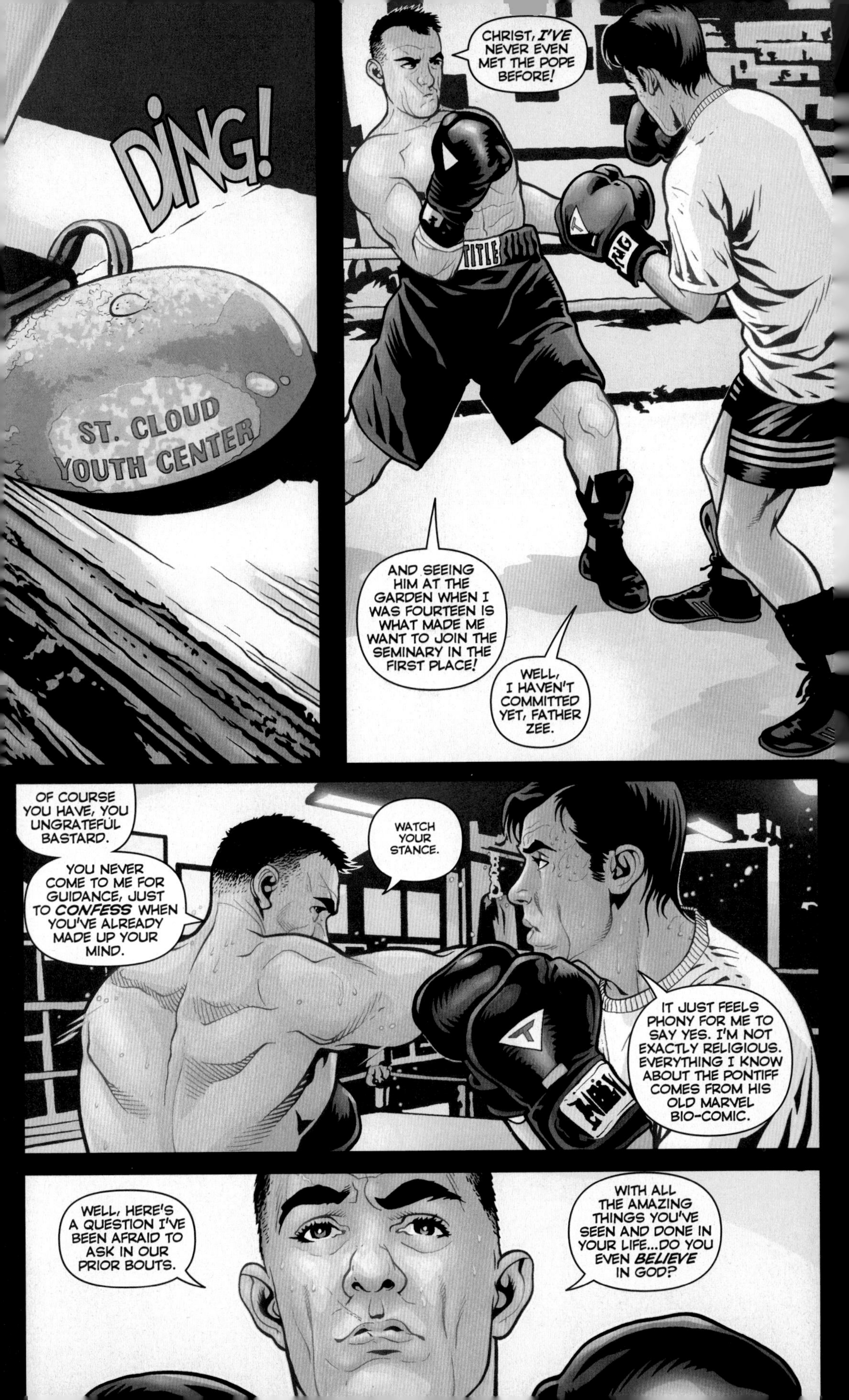
DING!
ST. CLOUD YOUTH CENTER
CHRIST, I'VE NEVER EVEN MET THE POPE BEFORE!
AND SEEING HIM AT THE GARDEN WHEN I WAS FOURTEEN IS WHAT MADE ME WANT TO JOIN THE SEMINARY IN THE FIRST PLACE!
WELL, I HAVEN'T COMMITTED YET, FATHER ZEE.
OF COURSE YOU HAVE, YOU UNGRATEFUL BASTARD.
YOU NEVER COME TO ME FOR GUIDANCE, JUST TO CONFESS WHEN YOU'VE ALREADY MADE UP YOUR MIND.
WATCH YOUR STANCE.
IT JUST FEELS PHONY FOR ME TO SAY YES. I'M NOT EXACTLY RELIGIOUS. EVERYTHING I KNOW ABOUT THE PONTIFF COMES FROM HIS OLD MARVEL BIO-COMIC.
WELL, HERE'S A QUESTION I'VE BEEN AFRAID TO ASK IN OUR PRIOR BOUTS.
WITH ALL THE AMAZING THINGS YOU'VE SEEN AND DONE IN YOUR LIFE...DO YOU EVEN BELIEVE IN GOD?

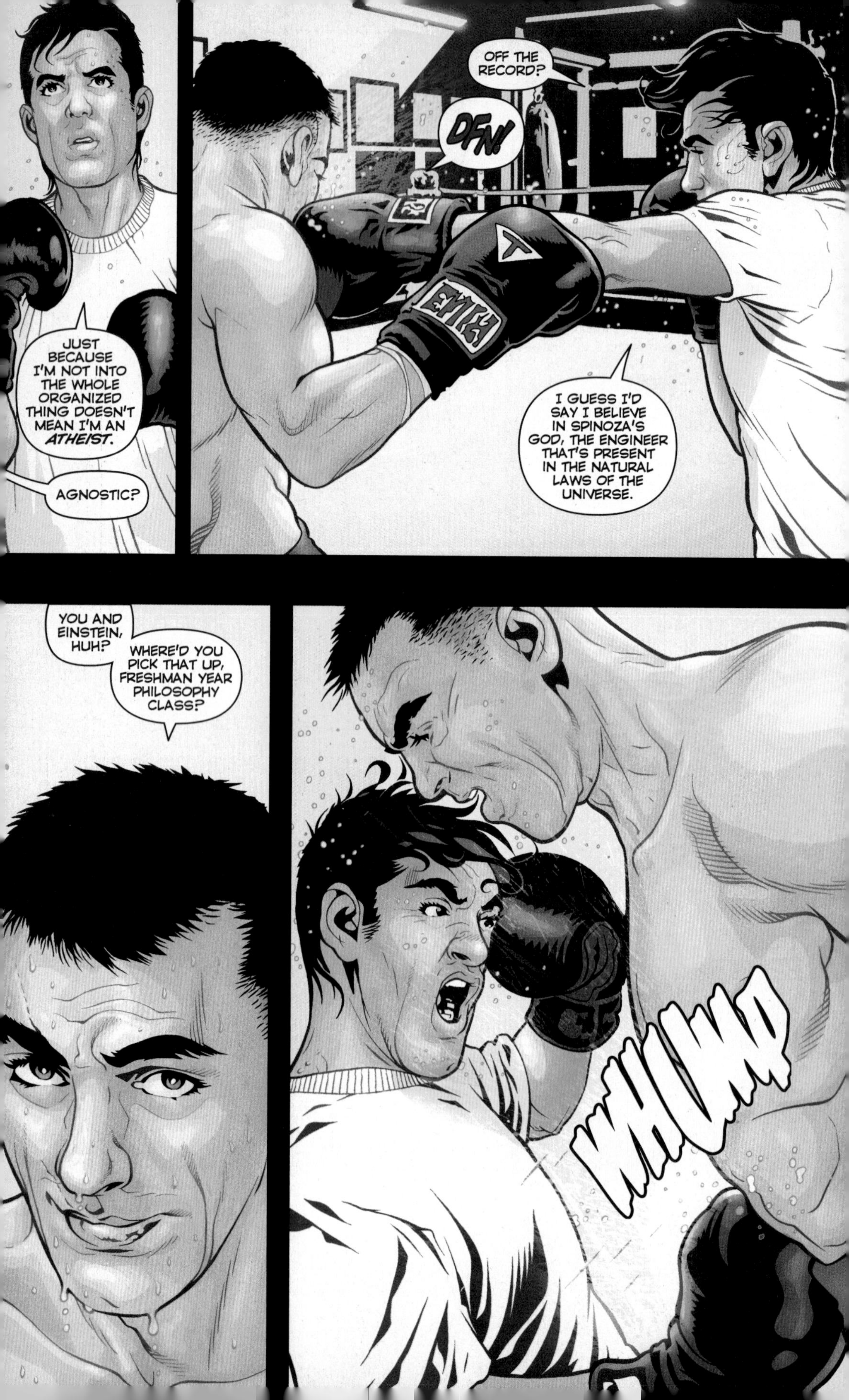

OFF THE RECORD?
DFN!
JUST BECAUSE I'M NOT INTO THE WHOLE ORGANIZED THING DOESN'T MEAN I'M AN *ATHEIST*.
AGNOSTIC?
I GUESS I'D SAY I BELIEVE IN SPINOZA'S GOD, THE ENGINEER THAT'S PRESENT IN THE NATURAL LAWS OF THE UNIVERSE.
YOU AND EINSTEIN, HUH?
WHERE'D YOU PICK THAT UP, FRESHMAN YEAR PHILOSOPHY CLASS?
WHUMP

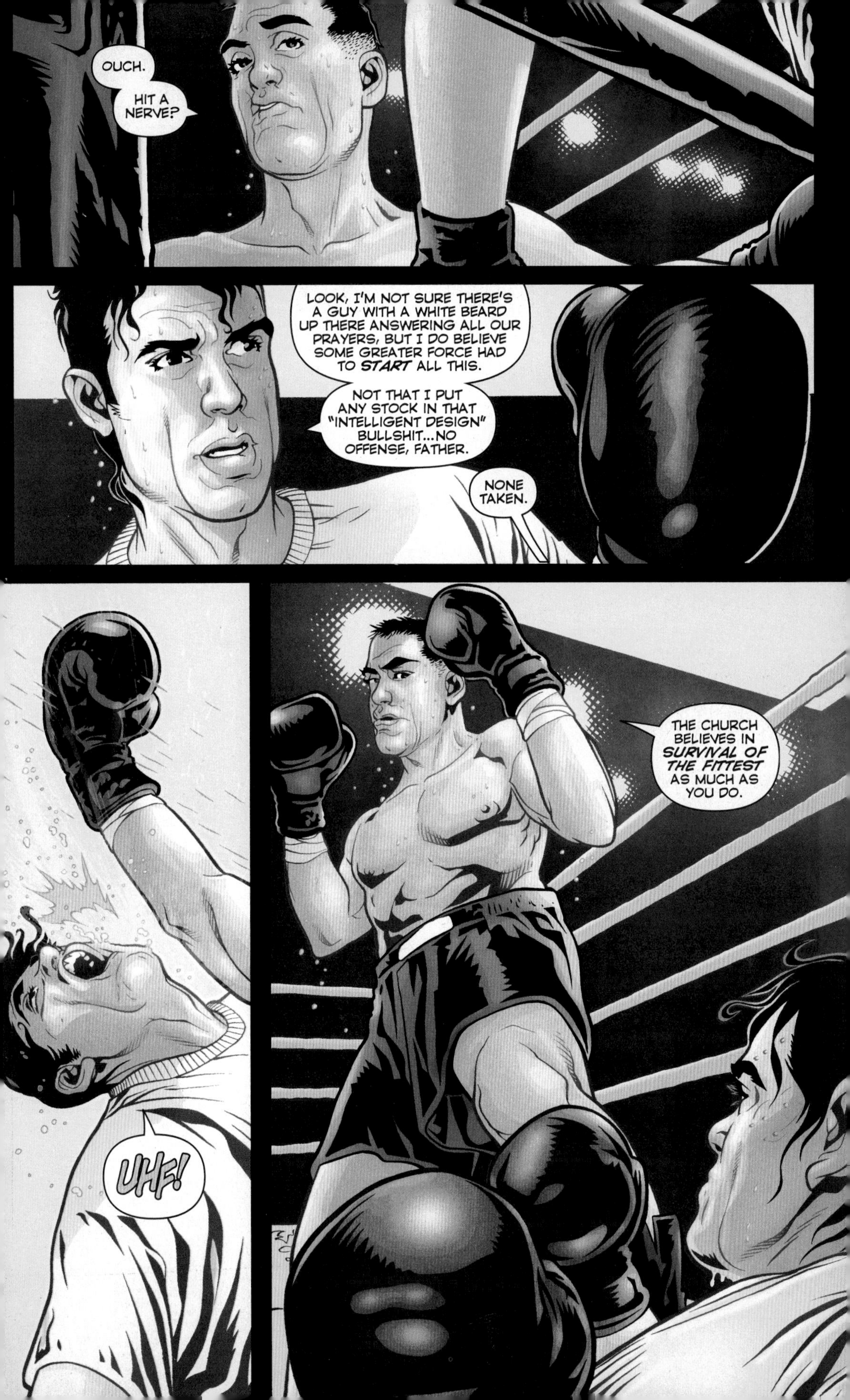
OUCH.
HIT A NERVE?
LOOK, I'M NOT SURE THERE'S A GUY WITH A WHITE BEARD UP THERE ANSWERING ALL OUR PRAYERS, BUT I DO BELIEVE SOME GREATER FORCE HAD TO START ALL THIS.
NOT THAT I PUT ANY STOCK IN THAT "INTELLIGENT DESIGN" BULLSHIT...NO OFFENSE, FATHER.
NONE TAKEN.
UHF!
THE CHURCH BELIEVES IN SURVIVAL OF THE FITTEST AS MUCH AS YOU DO.

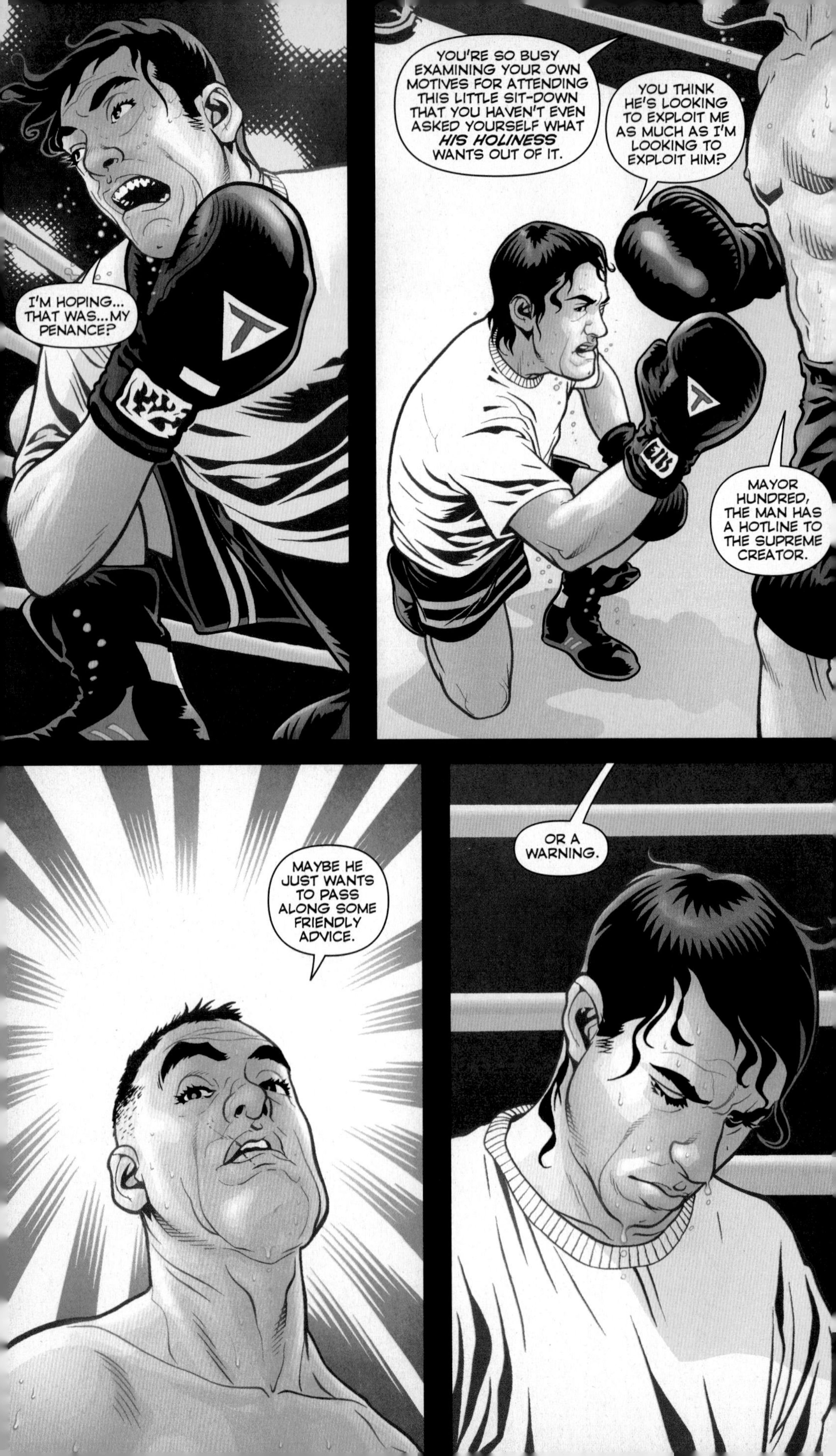
I'M HOPING... THAT WAS...MY PENANCE?
YOU'RE SO BUSY EXAMINING YOUR OWN MOTIVES FOR ATTENDING THIS LITTLE SIT-DOWN THAT YOU HAVEN'T EVEN ASKED YOURSELF WHAT HIS HOLINESS WANTS OUT OF IT.
YOU THINK HE'S LOOKING TO EXPLOIT ME AS MUCH AS I'M LOOKING TO EXPLOIT HIM?
MAYOR HUNDRED, THE MAN HAS A HOTLINE TO THE SUPREME CREATOR.
MAYBE HE JUST WANTS TO PASS ALONG SOME FRIENDLY ADVICE.
OR A WARNING.

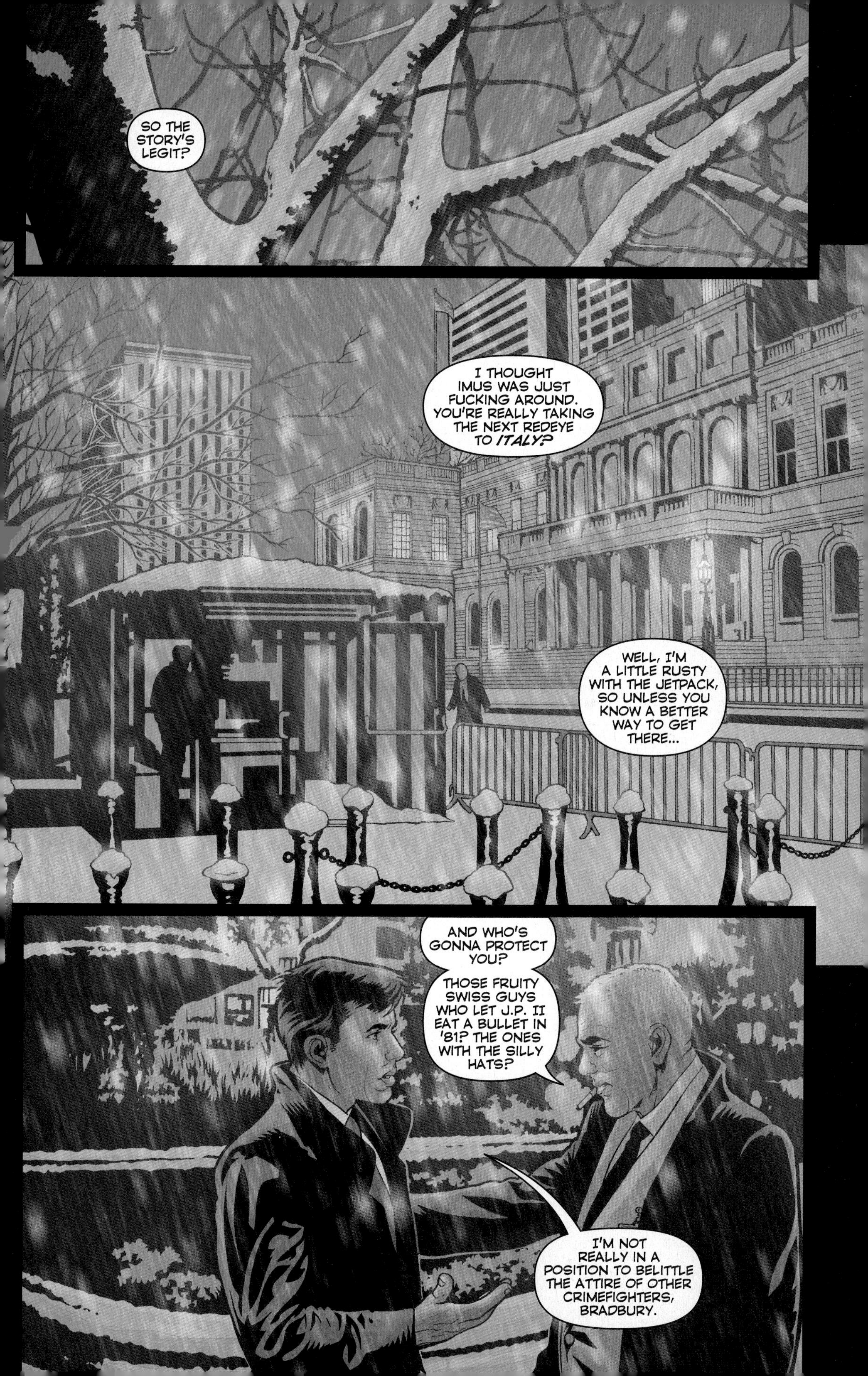
SO THE STORY'S LEGIT?
I THOUGHT IMUS WAS JUST FUCKING AROUND. YOU'RE REALLY TAKING THE NEXT REDEYE TO *ITALY?*
WELL, I'M A LITTLE RUSTY WITH THE JETPACK, SO UNLESS YOU KNOW A BETTER WAY TO GET THERE...
AND WHO'S GONNA PROTECT YOU?
THOSE FRUITY SWISS GUYS WHO LET J.P. II EAT A BULLET IN '81? THE ONES WITH THE SILLY HATS?
I'M NOT REALLY IN A POSITION TO BELITTLE THE ATTIRE OF OTHER CRIMEFIGHTERS, BRADBURY.

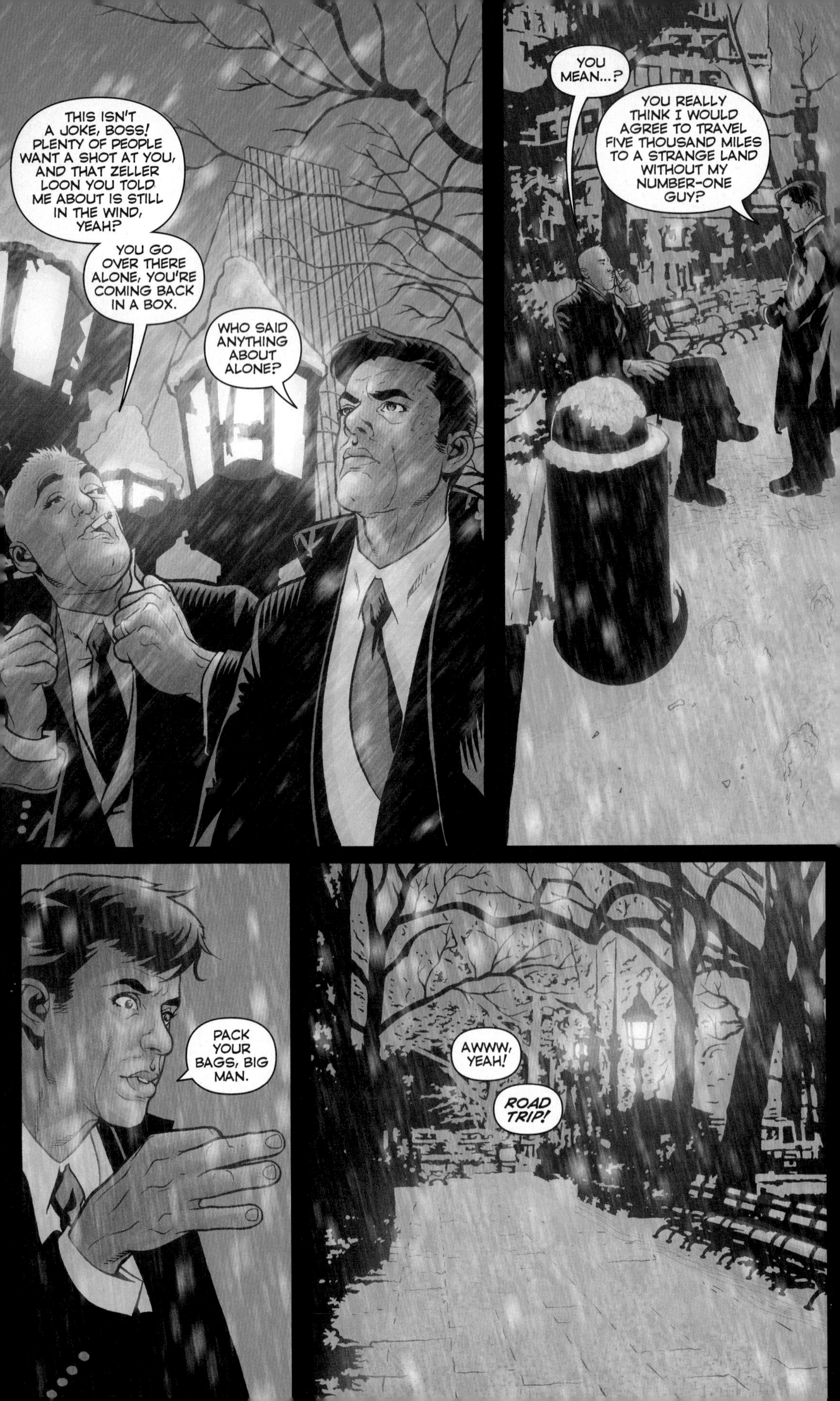
THIS ISN'T A JOKE, BOSS! PLENTY OF PEOPLE WANT A SHOT AT YOU, AND THAT ZELLER LOON YOU TOLD ME ABOUT IS STILL IN THE WIND, YEAH?
YOU GO OVER THERE ALONE, YOU'RE COMING BACK IN A BOX.
WHO SAID ANYTHING ABOUT ALONE?
YOU MEAN...?
YOU REALLY THINK I WOULD AGREE TO TRAVEL FIVE THOUSAND MILES TO A STRANGE LAND WITHOUT MY NUMBER-ONE GUY?
PACK YOUR BAGS, BIG MAN.
AWWW, YEAH!
ROAD TRIP!

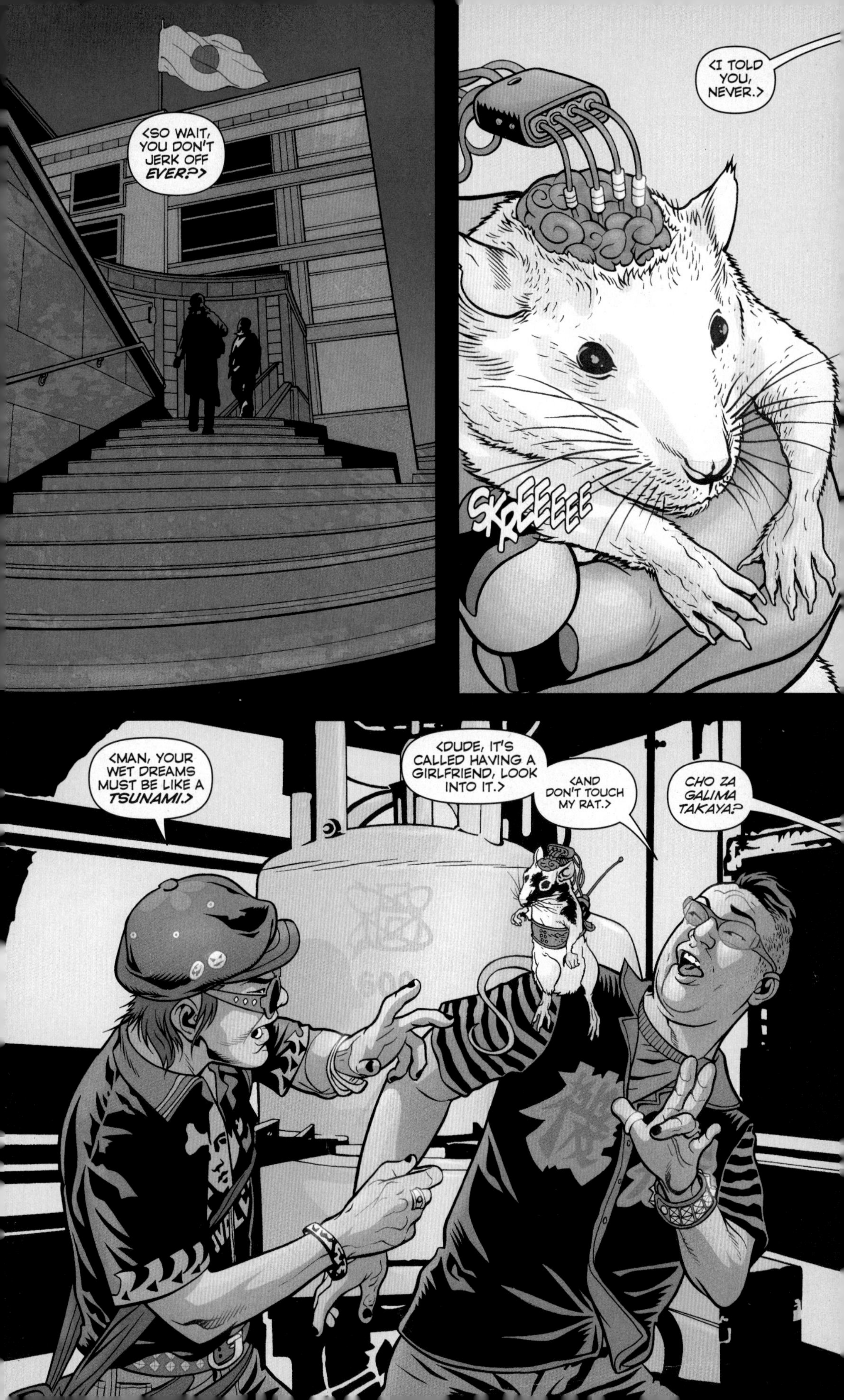
<SO WAIT, YOU DON'T JERK OFF *EVER?*>
<I TOLD YOU, NEVER.>
SKREEEEEE
<MAN, YOUR WET DREAMS MUST BE LIKE A *TSUNAMI.*>
<DUDE, IT'S CALLED HAVING A GIRLFRIEND, LOOK INTO IT.>
<AND DON'T TOUCH MY RAT.>
CHO ZA GALIMA TAKAYA?

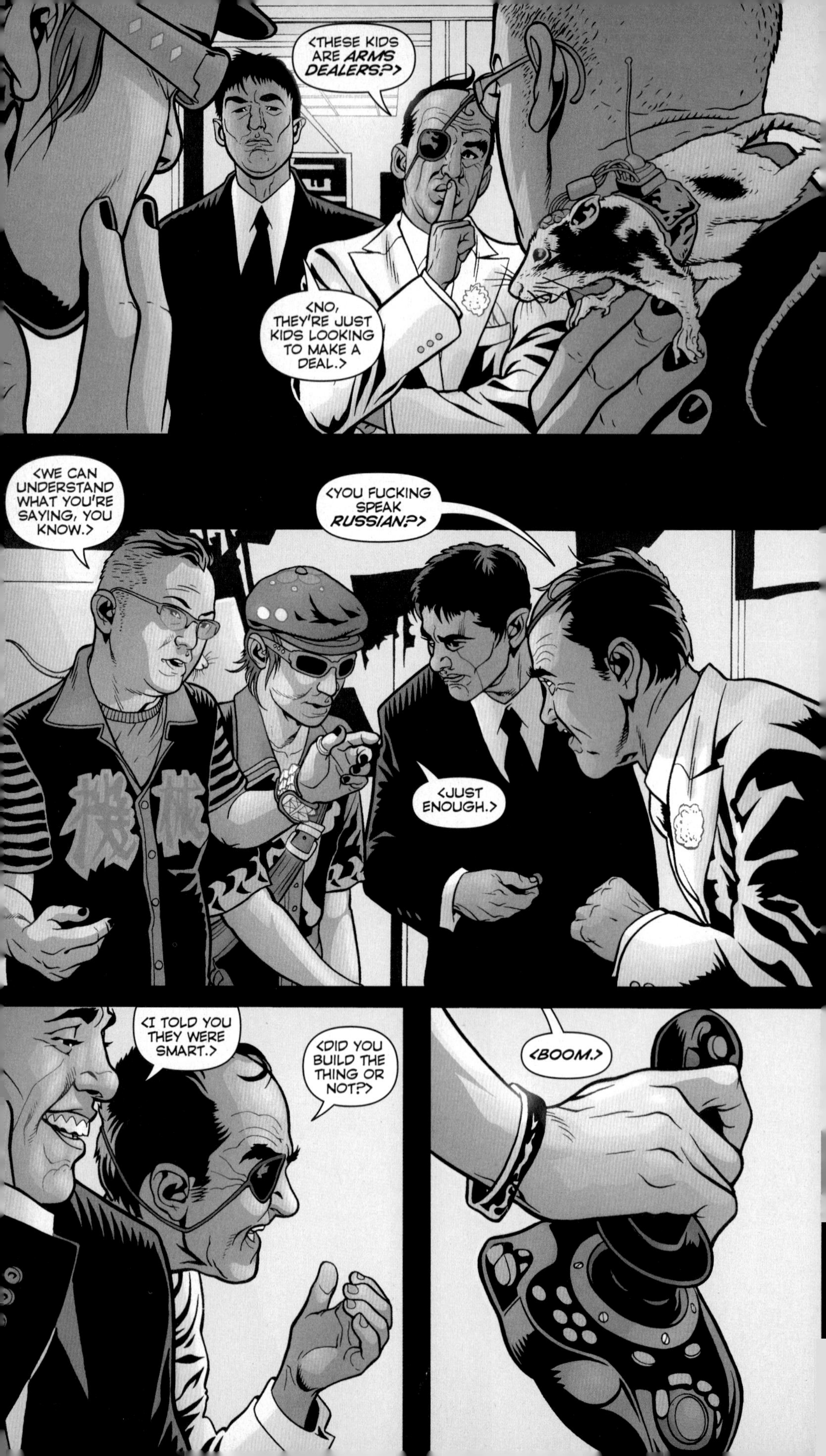

<THESE KIDS ARE ARMS DEALERS?>
<NO, THEY'RE JUST KIDS LOOKING TO MAKE A DEAL.>
<WE CAN UNDERSTAND WHAT YOU'RE SAYING, YOU KNOW.>
<YOU FUCKING SPEAK RUSSIAN?>
<JUST ENOUGH.>
機械
<I TOLD YOU THEY WERE SMART.>
<DID YOU BUILD THE THING OR NOT?>
<BOOM.>

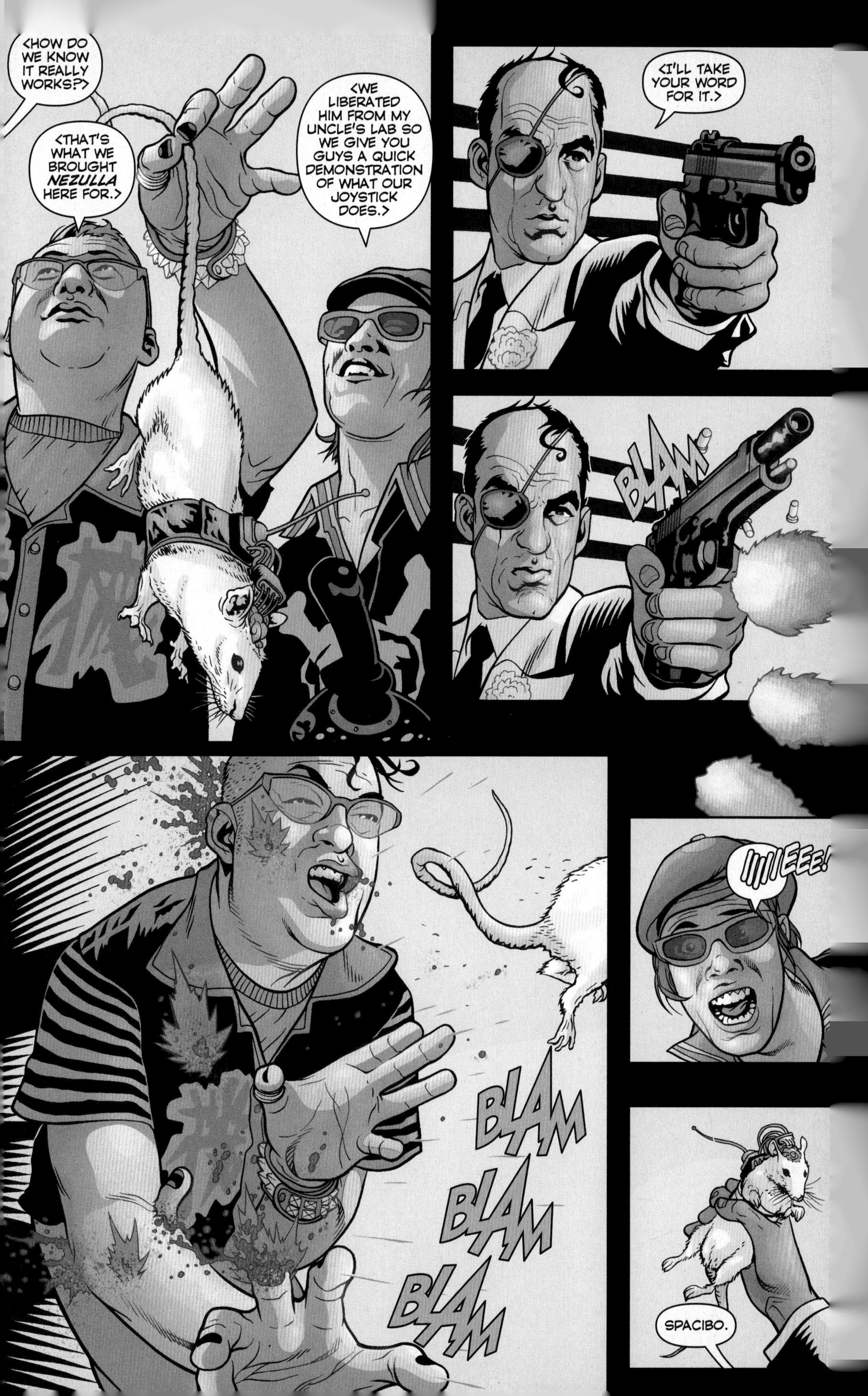
<HOW DO WE KNOW IT REALLY WORKS?>
<THAT'S WHAT WE BROUGHT **NEZULLA** HERE FOR.>
<WE LIBERATED HIM FROM MY UNCLE'S LAB SO WE GIVE YOU GUYS A QUICK DEMONSTRATION OF WHAT OUR JOYSTICK DOES.>
<I'LL TAKE YOUR WORD FOR IT.>
BLAM
BLAM
BLAM
BLAM
IIIIIEEE!
SPACIBO.

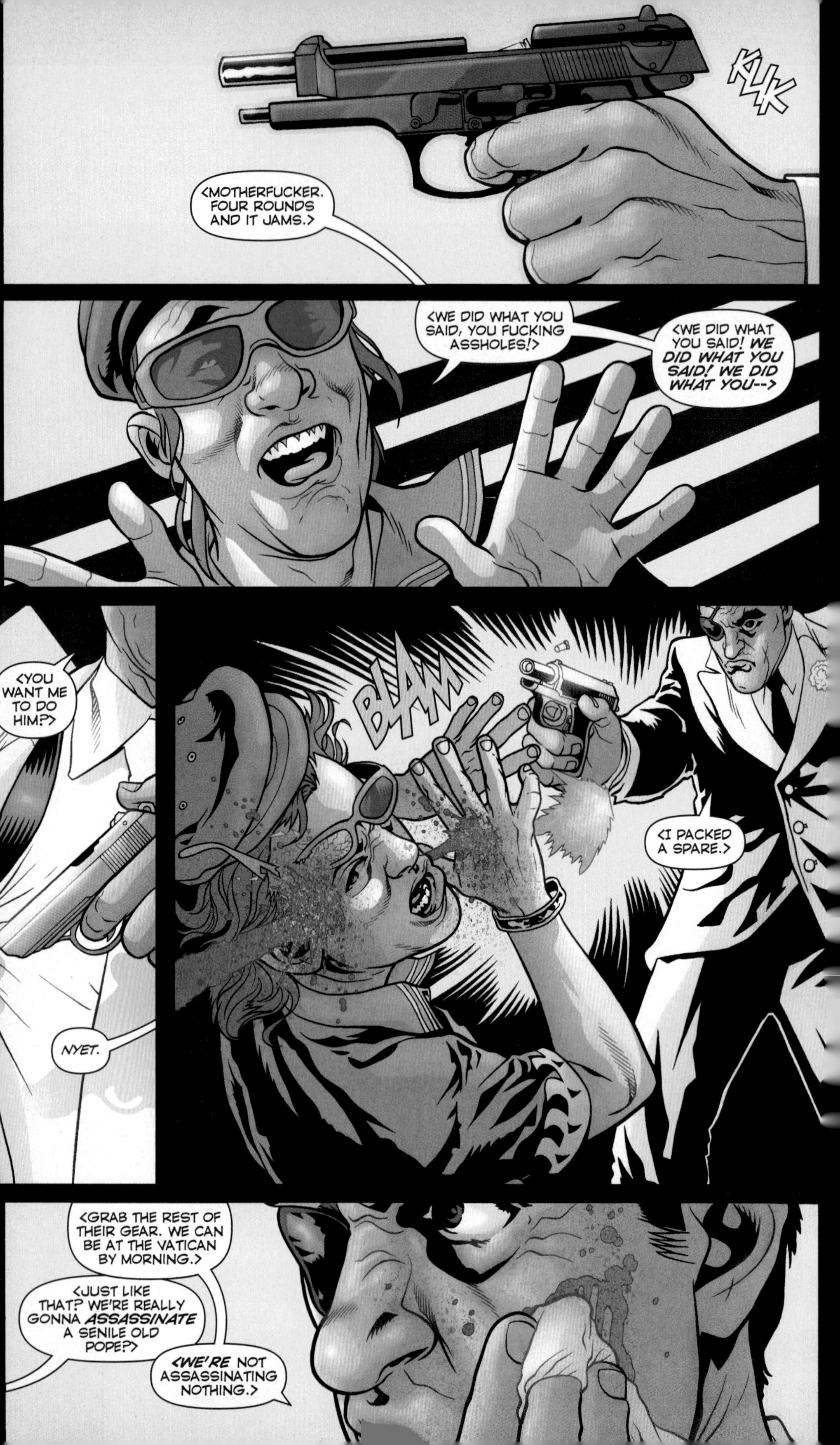

KLIK
<MOTHERFUCKER. FOUR ROUNDS AND IT JAMS.>
<WE DID WHAT YOU SAID, YOU FUCKING ASSHOLES!>
<WE DID WHAT YOU SAID! WE DID WHAT YOU SAID! WE DID WHAT YOU-->
<YOU WANT ME TO DO HIM?>
NYET.
BLAM
<I PACKED A SPARE.>
<GRAB THE REST OF THEIR GEAR. WE CAN BE AT THE VATICAN BY MORNING.>
<JUST LIKE THAT? WE'RE REALLY GONNA ASSASSINATE A SENILE OLD POPE?>
<WE'RE NOT ASSASSINATING NOTHING.>

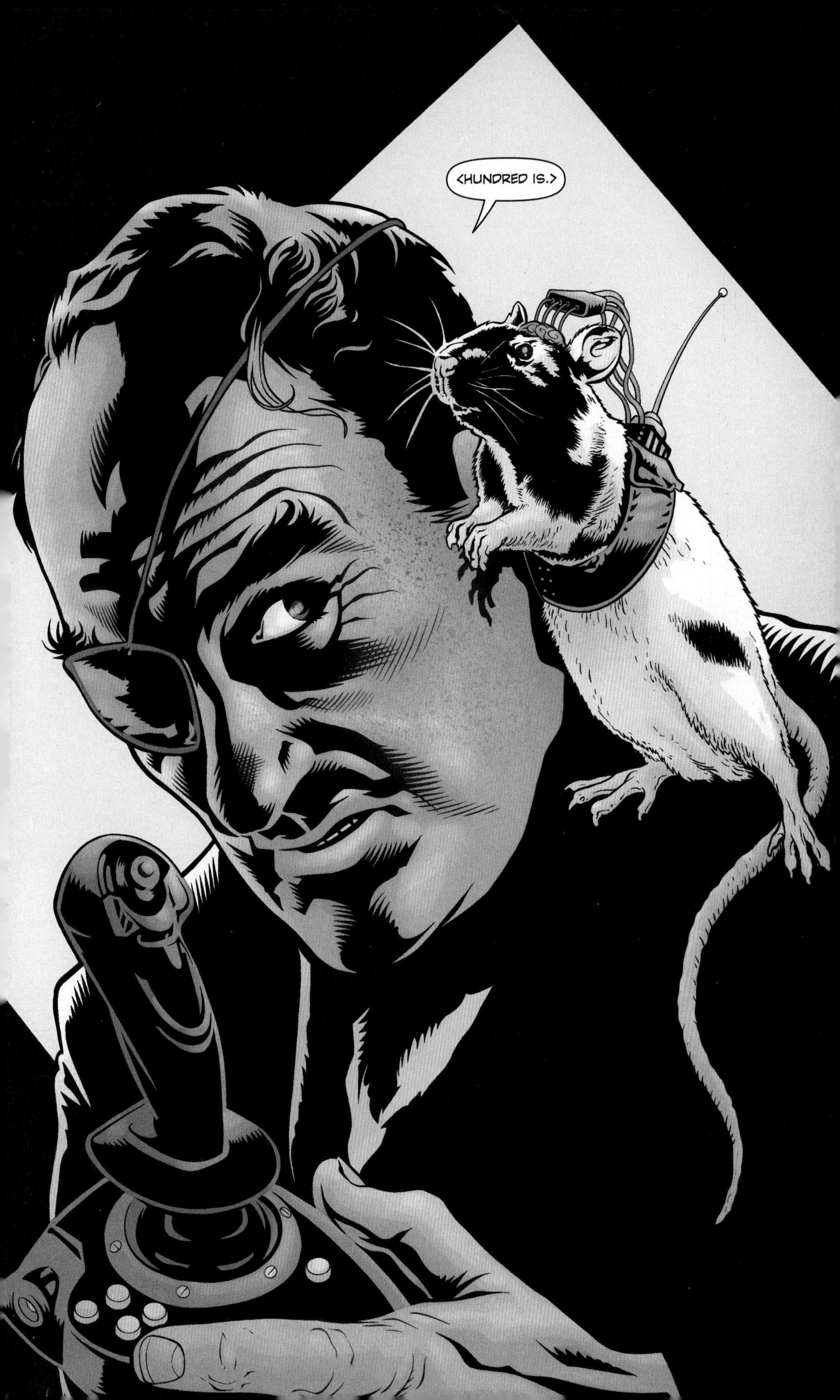
<HUNDRED IS.>

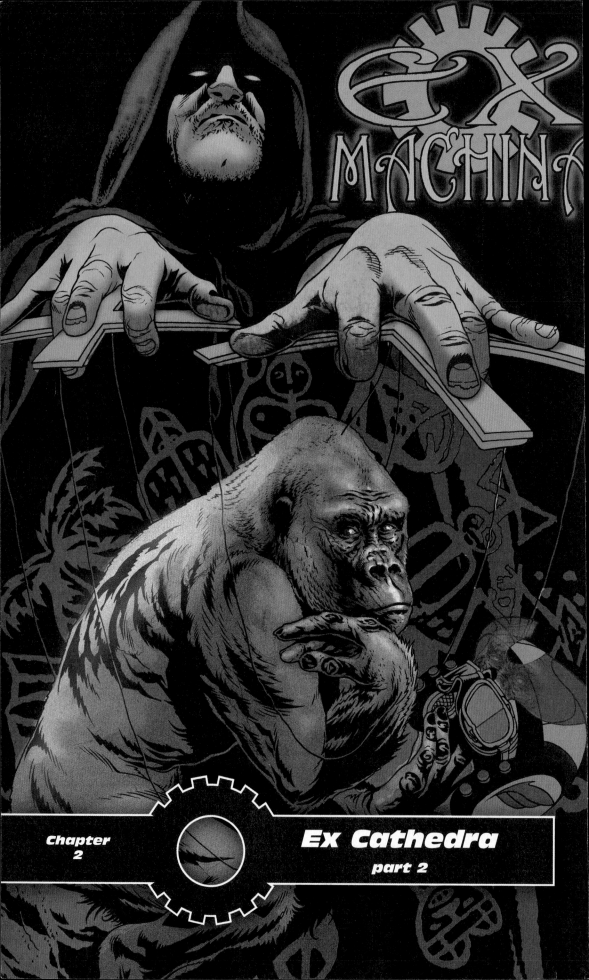

GOD MACHINA

Chapter 2

Ex Cathedra

part 2

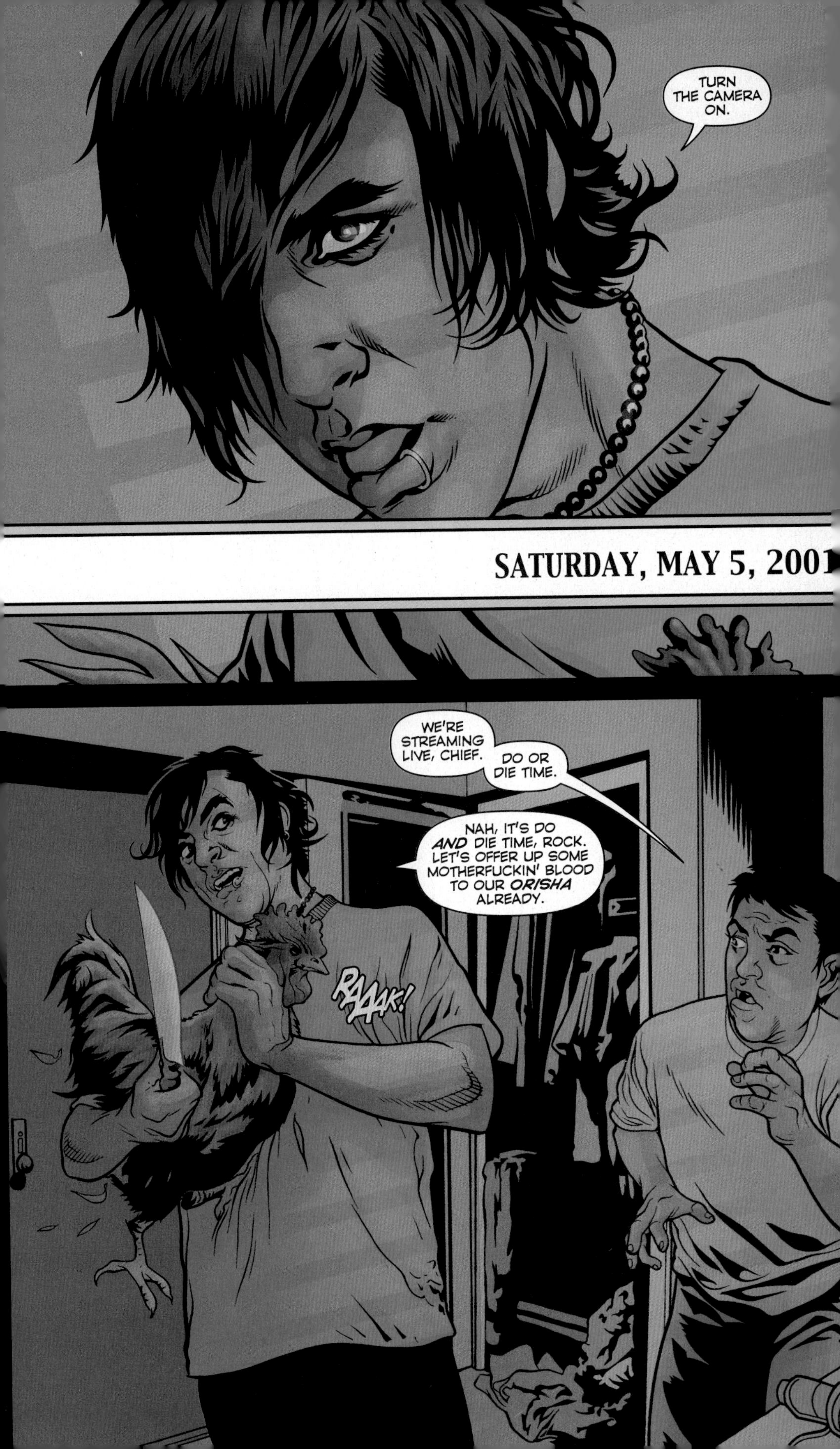
TURN THE CAMERA ON.
SATURDAY, MAY 5, 2001
WE'RE STREAMING LIVE, CHIEF.
DO OR DIE TIME.
NAH, IT'S DO AND DIE TIME, ROCK. LET'S OFFER UP SOME MOTHERFUCKIN' BLOOD TO OUR ORISHA ALREADY.
RAAAK!

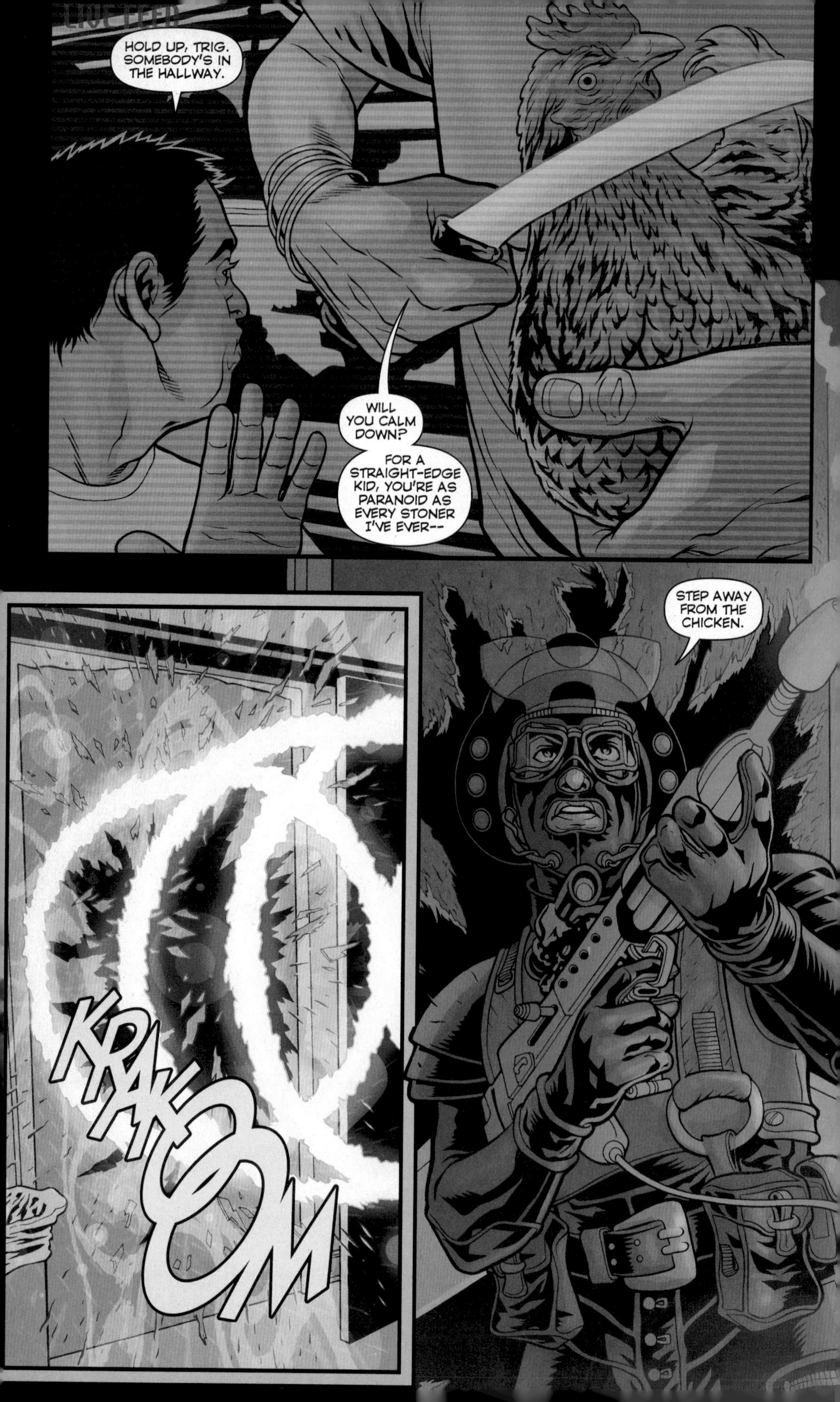
HOLD UP, TRIG. SOMEBODY'S IN THE HALLWAY.
WILL YOU CALM DOWN?
FOR A STRAIGHT-EDGE KID, YOU'RE AS PARANOID AS EVERY STONER I'VE EVER--
KRAKOOM
STEP AWAY FROM THE CHICKEN.

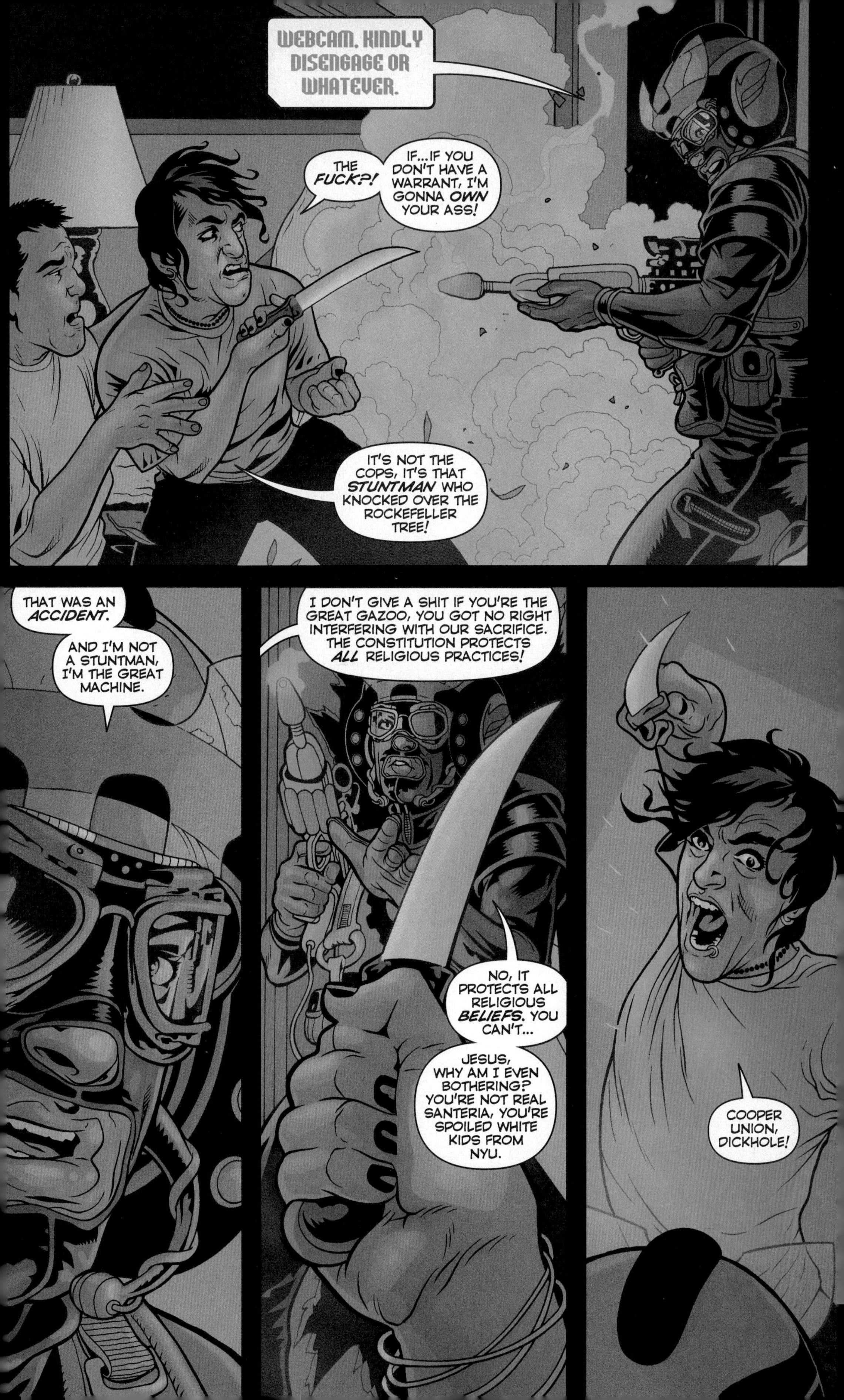
WEBCAM, KINDLY DISENGAGE OR WHATEVER.
THE FUCK?!
IF...IF YOU DON'T HAVE A WARRANT, I'M GONNA OWN YOUR ASS!
IT'S NOT THE COPS, IT'S THAT STUNTMAN WHO KNOCKED OVER THE ROCKEFELLER TREE!
THAT WAS AN ACCIDENT.
AND I'M NOT A STUNTMAN, I'M THE GREAT MACHINE.
I DON'T GIVE A SHIT IF YOU'RE THE GREAT GAZOO, YOU GOT NO RIGHT INTERFERING WITH OUR SACRIFICE. THE CONSTITUTION PROTECTS ALL RELIGIOUS PRACTICES!
NO, IT PROTECTS ALL RELIGIOUS BELIEFS. YOU CAN'T...
JESUS, WHY AM I EVEN BOTHERING? YOU'RE NOT REAL SANTERIA, YOU'RE SPOILED WHITE KIDS FROM NYU.
COOPER UNION, DICKHOLE!

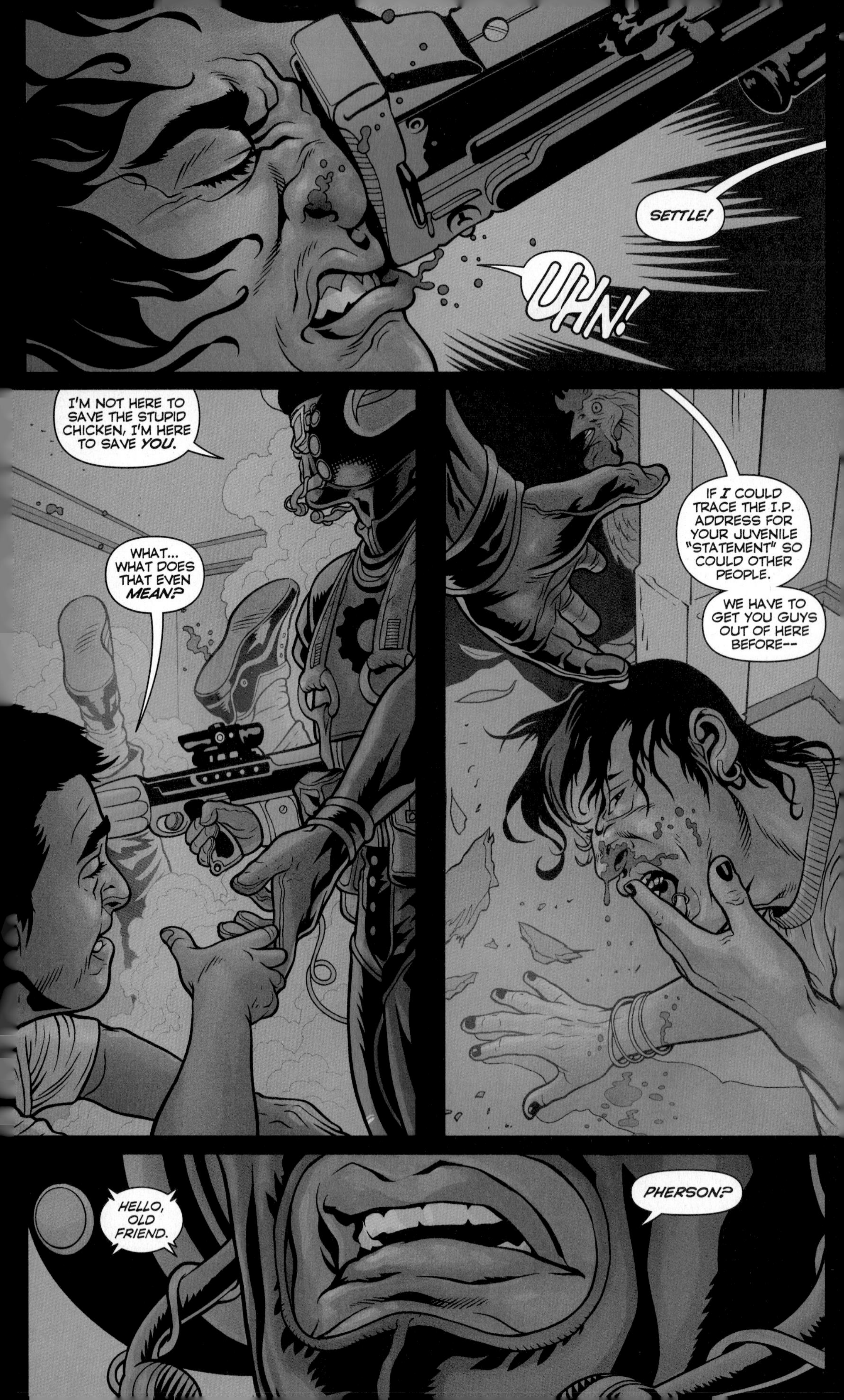
SETTLE!
UHN!
I'M NOT HERE TO SAVE THE STUPID CHICKEN, I'M HERE TO SAVE *YOU.*
WHAT... WHAT DOES THAT EVEN *MEAN?*
IF *I* COULD TRACE THE I.P. ADDRESS FOR YOUR JUVENILE "STATEMENT" SO COULD OTHER PEOPLE.
WE HAVE TO GET YOU GUYS OUT OF HERE BEFORE--
HELLO, OLD FRIEND.
PHERSON?

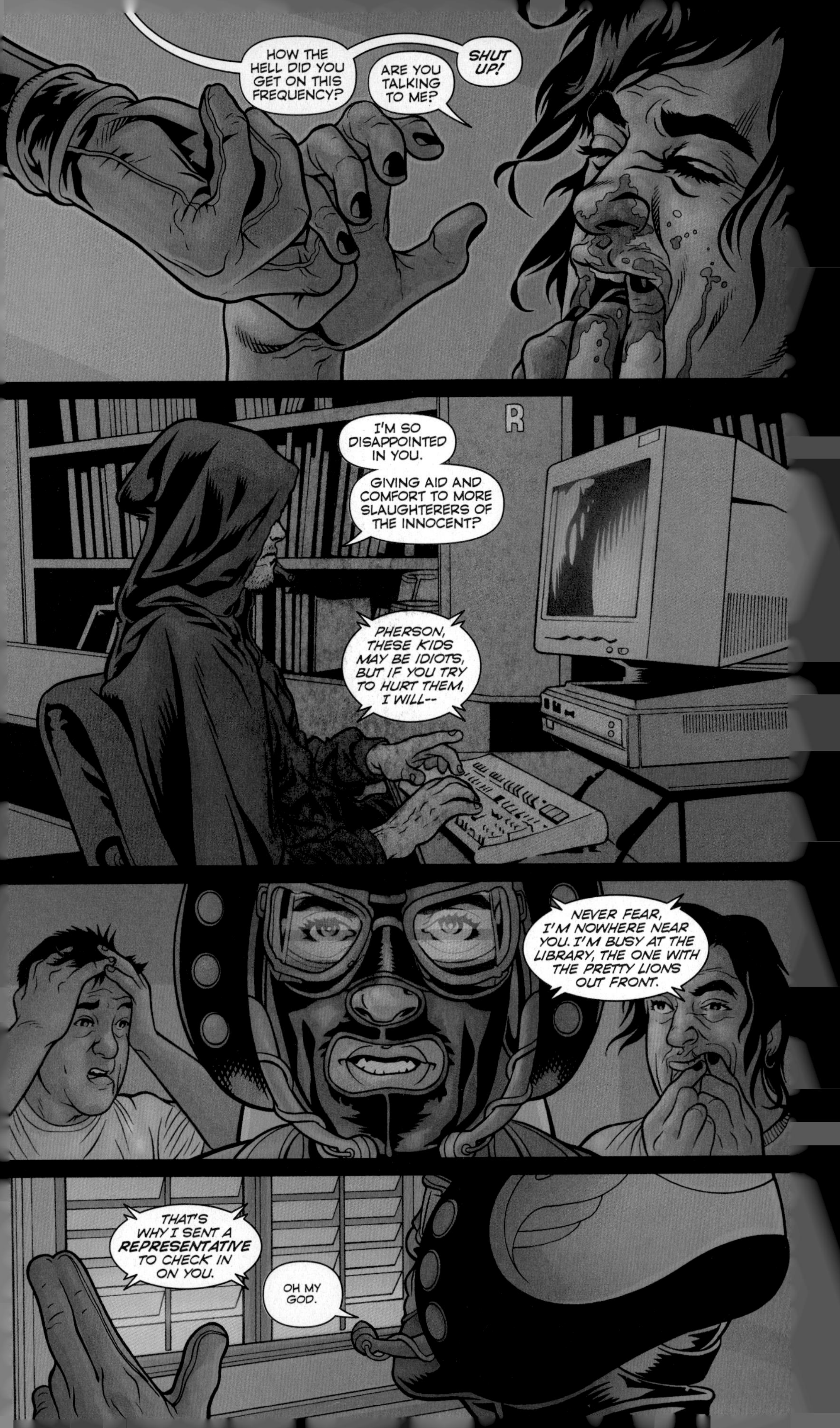
HOW THE HELL DID YOU GET ON THIS FREQUENCY?
ARE YOU TALKING TO ME?
SHUT UP!
R
I'M SO DISAPPOINTED IN YOU.
GIVING AID AND COMFORT TO MORE SLAUGHTERERS OF THE INNOCENT?
PHERSON, THESE KIDS MAY BE IDIOTS, BUT IF YOU TRY TO HURT THEM, I WILL--
NEVER FEAR, I'M NOWHERE NEAR YOU. I'M BUSY AT THE LIBRARY, THE ONE WITH THE PRETTY LIONS OUT FRONT.
THAT'S WHY I SENT A REPRESENTATIVE TO CHECK IN ON YOU.
OH MY GOD.

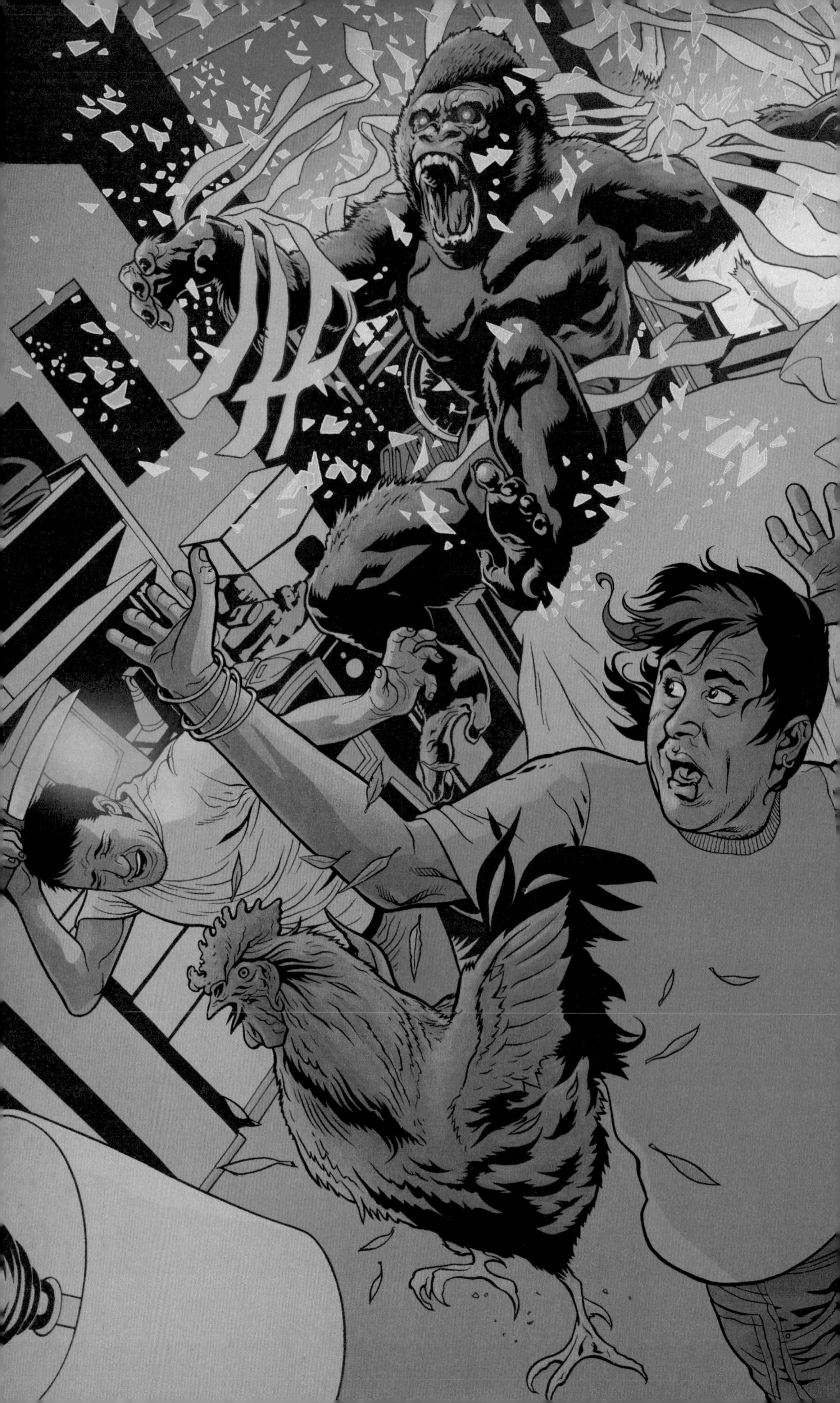

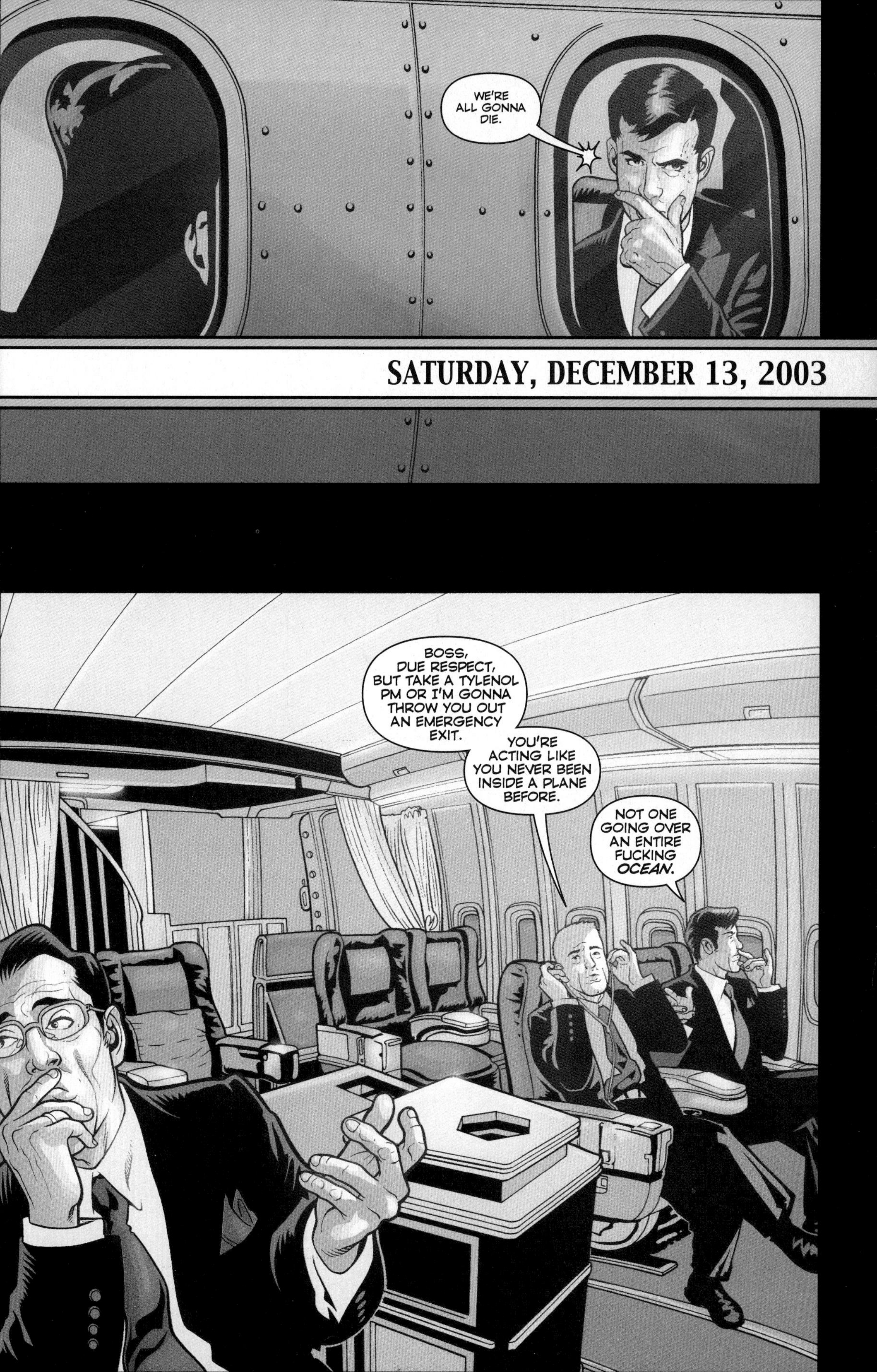
WE'RE ALL GONNA DIE.
SATURDAY, DECEMBER 13, 2003
BOSS, DUE RESPECT, BUT TAKE A TYLENOL PM OR I'M GONNA THROW YOU OUT AN EMERGENCY EXIT.
YOU'RE ACTING LIKE YOU NEVER BEEN INSIDE A PLANE BEFORE.
NOT ONE GOING OVER AN ENTIRE FUCKING *OCEAN*.

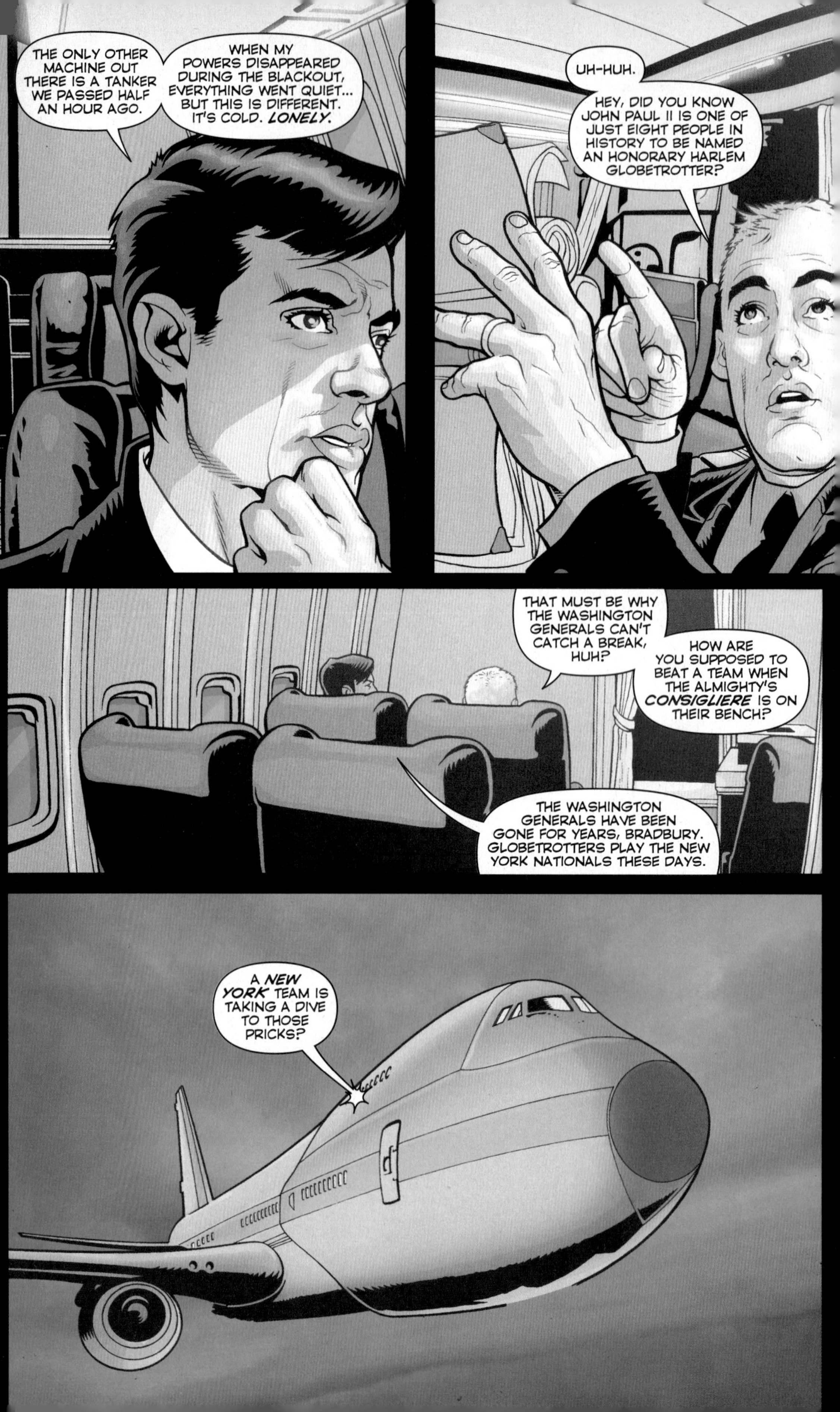
THE ONLY OTHER MACHINE OUT THERE IS A TANKER WE PASSED HALF AN HOUR AGO.
WHEN MY POWERS DISAPPEARED DURING THE BLACKOUT, EVERYTHING WENT QUIET... BUT THIS IS DIFFERENT. IT'S COLD. *LONELY.*
UH-HUH.
HEY, DID YOU KNOW JOHN PAUL II IS ONE OF JUST EIGHT PEOPLE IN HISTORY TO BE NAMED AN HONORARY HARLEM GLOBETROTTER?
THAT MUST BE WHY THE WASHINGTON GENERALS CAN'T CATCH A BREAK, HUH?
HOW ARE YOU SUPPOSED TO BEAT A TEAM WHEN THE ALMIGHTY'S *CONSIGLIERE* IS ON THEIR BENCH?
THE WASHINGTON GENERALS HAVE BEEN GONE FOR YEARS, BRADBURY. GLOBETROTTERS PLAY THE NEW YORK NATIONALS THESE DAYS.
A *NEW YORK* TEAM IS TAKING A DIVE TO THOSE PRICKS?

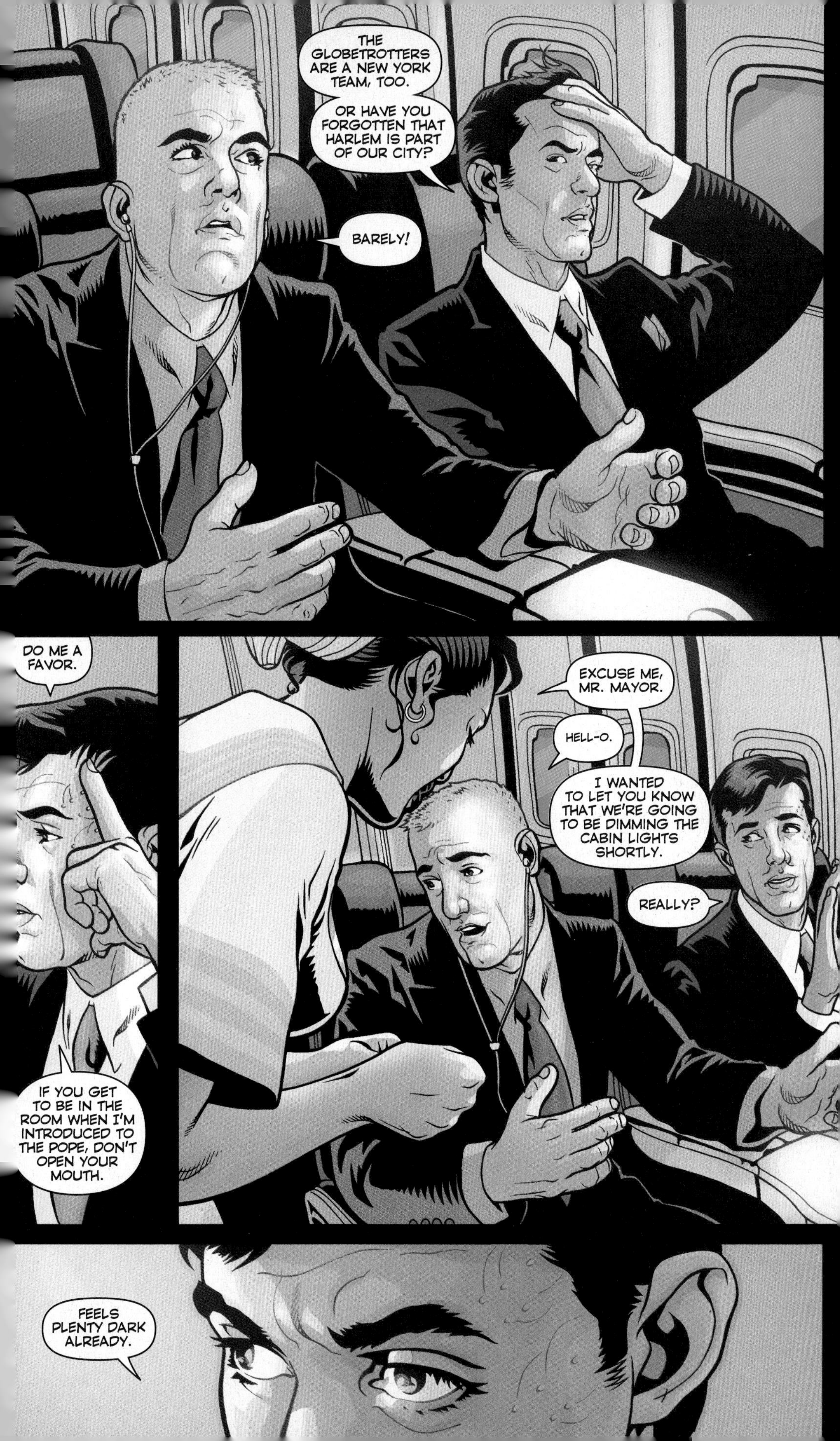
THE GLOBETROTTERS ARE A NEW YORK TEAM, TOO.
OR HAVE YOU FORGOTTEN THAT HARLEM IS PART OF OUR CITY?
BARELY!
DO ME A FAVOR.
IF YOU GET TO BE IN THE ROOM WHEN I'M INTRODUCED TO THE POPE, DON'T OPEN YOUR MOUTH.
EXCUSE ME, MR. MAYOR.
HELL-O.
I WANTED TO LET YOU KNOW THAT WE'RE GOING TO BE DIMMING THE CABIN LIGHTS SHORTLY.
REALLY?
FEELS PLENTY DARK ALREADY.

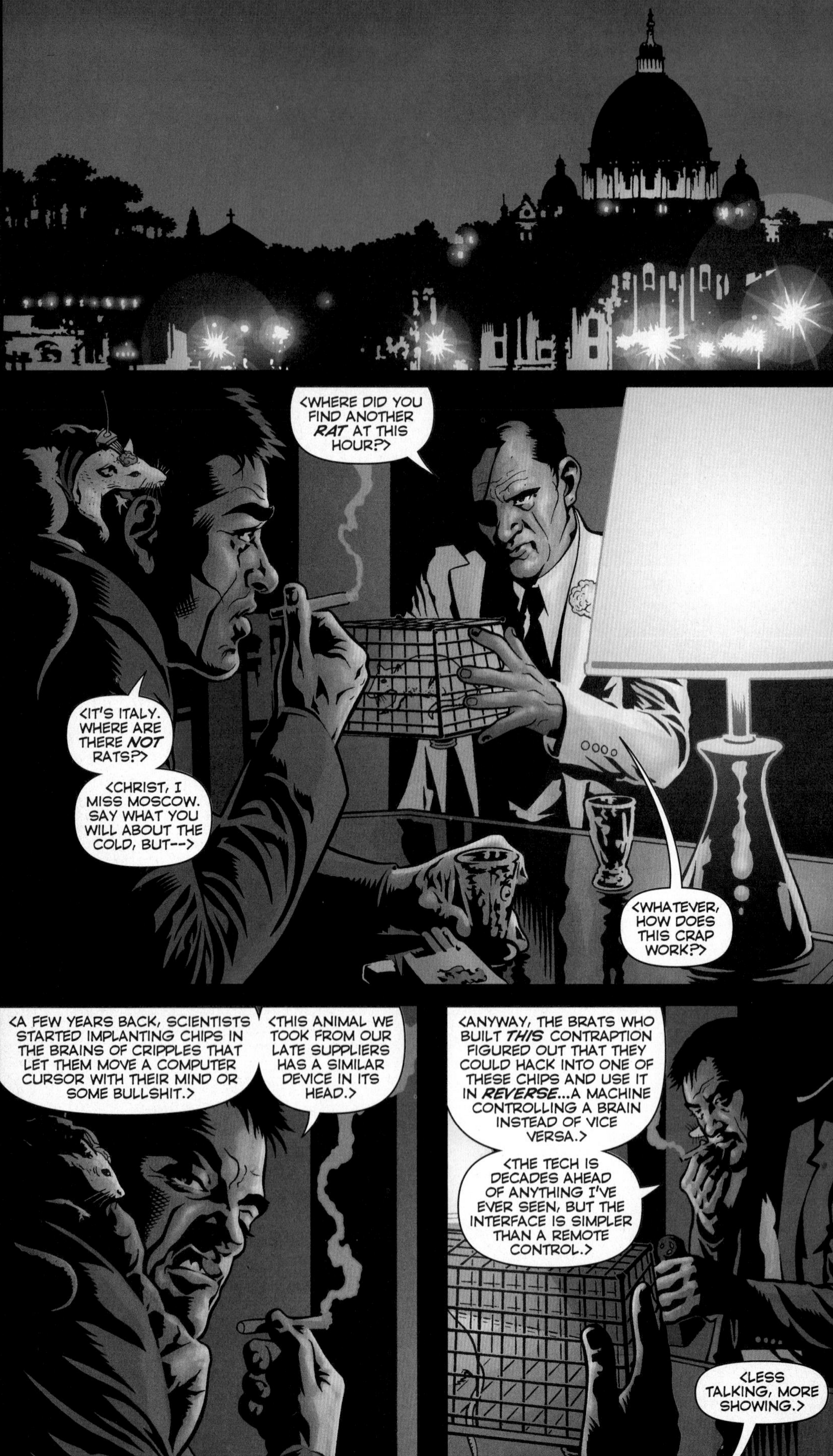
<WHERE DID YOU FIND ANOTHER *RAT* AT THIS HOUR?>
<IT'S ITALY. WHERE ARE THERE *NOT* RATS?>
<CHRIST, I MISS MOSCOW. SAY WHAT YOU WILL ABOUT THE COLD, BUT-->
<WHATEVER, HOW DOES THIS CRAP WORK?>
<A FEW YEARS BACK, SCIENTISTS STARTED IMPLANTING CHIPS IN THE BRAINS OF CRIPPLES THAT LET THEM MOVE A COMPUTER CURSOR WITH THEIR MIND OR SOME BULLSHIT.>
<THIS ANIMAL WE TOOK FROM OUR LATE SUPPLIERS HAS A SIMILAR DEVICE IN ITS HEAD.>
<ANYWAY, THE BRATS WHO BUILT *THIS* CONTRAPTION FIGURED OUT THAT THEY COULD HACK INTO ONE OF THESE CHIPS AND USE IT IN *REVERSE*...A MACHINE CONTROLLING A BRAIN INSTEAD OF VICE VERSA.>
<THE TECH IS DECADES AHEAD OF ANYTHING I'VE EVER SEEN, BUT THE INTERFACE IS SIMPLER THAN A REMOTE CONTROL.>
<LESS TALKING, MORE SHOWING.>

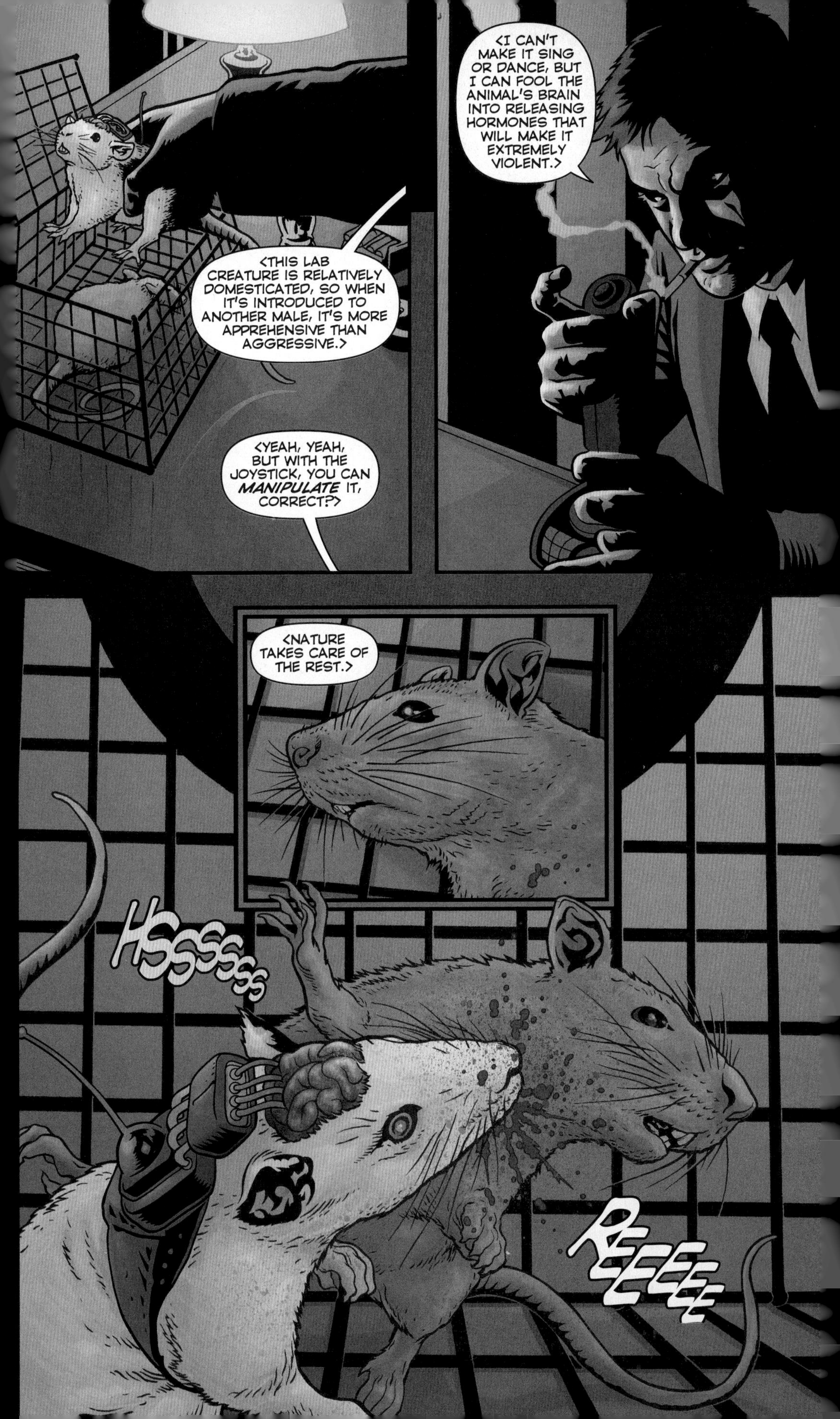
<THIS LAB CREATURE IS RELATIVELY DOMESTICATED, SO WHEN IT'S INTRODUCED TO ANOTHER MALE, IT'S MORE APPREHENSIVE THAN AGGRESSIVE.>
<YEAH, YEAH, BUT WITH THE JOYSTICK, YOU CAN *MANIPULATE* IT, CORRECT?>
<I CAN'T MAKE IT SING OR DANCE, BUT I CAN FOOL THE ANIMAL'S BRAIN INTO RELEASING HORMONES THAT WILL MAKE IT EXTREMELY VIOLENT.>
<NATURE TAKES CARE OF THE REST.>
HSSSSSS
REEEEEE

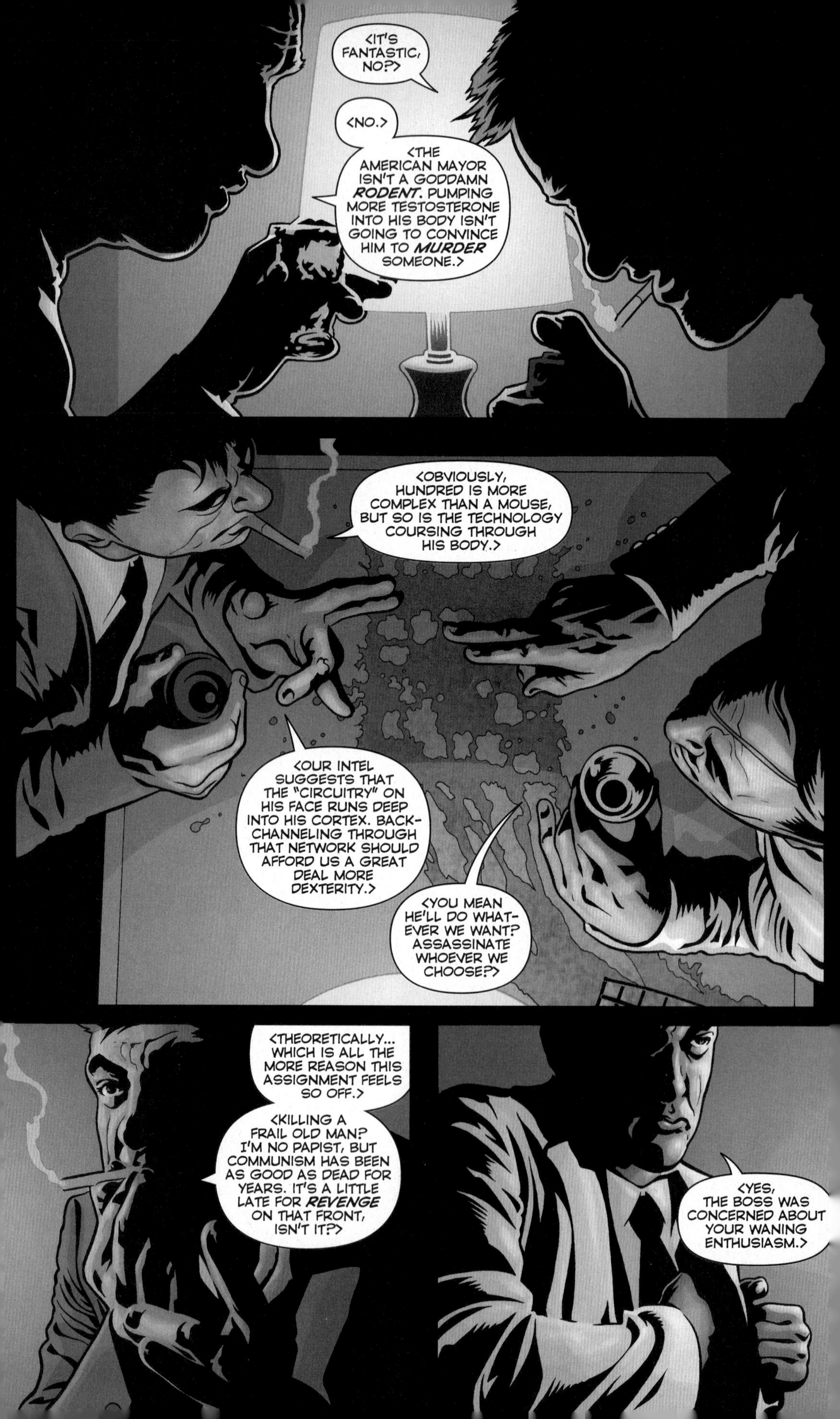
<IT'S FANTASTIC, NO?>
<NO.>
<THE AMERICAN MAYOR ISN'T A GODDAMN ***RODENT***. PUMPING MORE TESTOSTERONE INTO HIS BODY ISN'T GOING TO CONVINCE HIM TO ***MURDER*** SOMEONE.>
<OBVIOUSLY, HUNDRED IS MORE COMPLEX THAN A MOUSE, BUT SO IS THE TECHNOLOGY COURSING THROUGH HIS BODY.>
<OUR INTEL SUGGESTS THAT THE "CIRCUITRY" ON HIS FACE RUNS DEEP INTO HIS CORTEX. BACK-CHANNELING THROUGH THAT NETWORK SHOULD AFFORD US A GREAT DEAL MORE DEXTERITY.>
<YOU MEAN HE'LL DO WHAT-EVER WE WANT? ASSASSINATE WHOEVER WE CHOOSE?>
<THEORETICALLY... WHICH IS ALL THE MORE REASON THIS ASSIGNMENT FEELS SO OFF.>
<KILLING A FRAIL OLD MAN? I'M NO PAPIST, BUT COMMUNISM HAS BEEN AS GOOD AS DEAD FOR YEARS. IT'S A LITTLE LATE FOR ***REVENGE*** ON THAT FRONT, ISN'T IT?>
<YES, THE BOSS WAS CONCERNED ABOUT YOUR WANING ENTHUSIASM.>

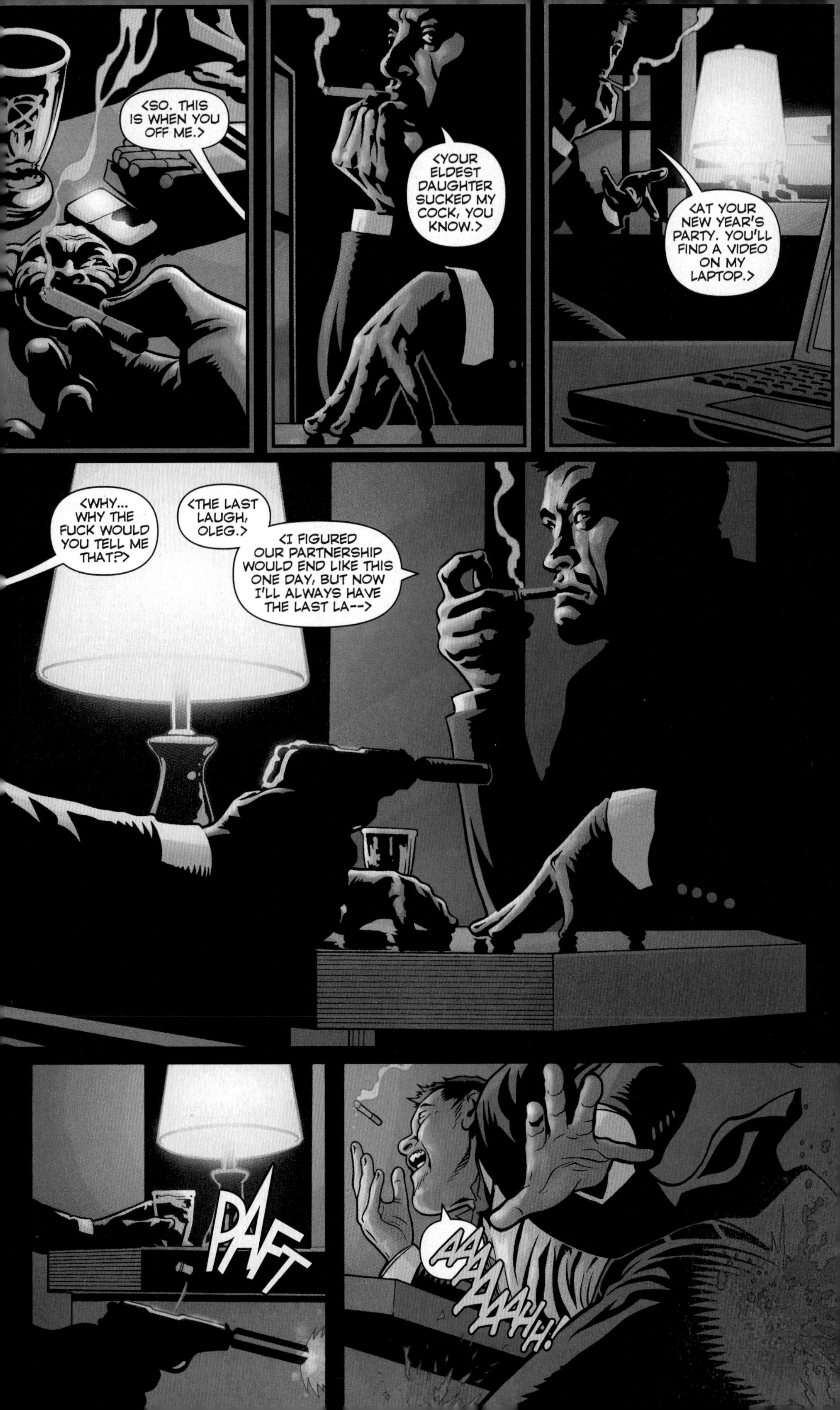

<SO. THIS IS WHEN YOU OFF ME.>
<YOUR ELDEST DAUGHTER SUCKED MY COCK, YOU KNOW.>
<AT YOUR NEW YEAR'S PARTY. YOU'LL FIND A VIDEO ON MY LAPTOP.>
<WHY... WHY THE FUCK WOULD YOU TELL ME THAT?>
<THE LAST LAUGH, OLEG.>
<I FIGURED OUR PARTNERSHIP WOULD END LIKE THIS ONE DAY, BUT NOW I'LL ALWAYS HAVE THE LAST LA-->
PAFT
AAAAAAAAAHH!

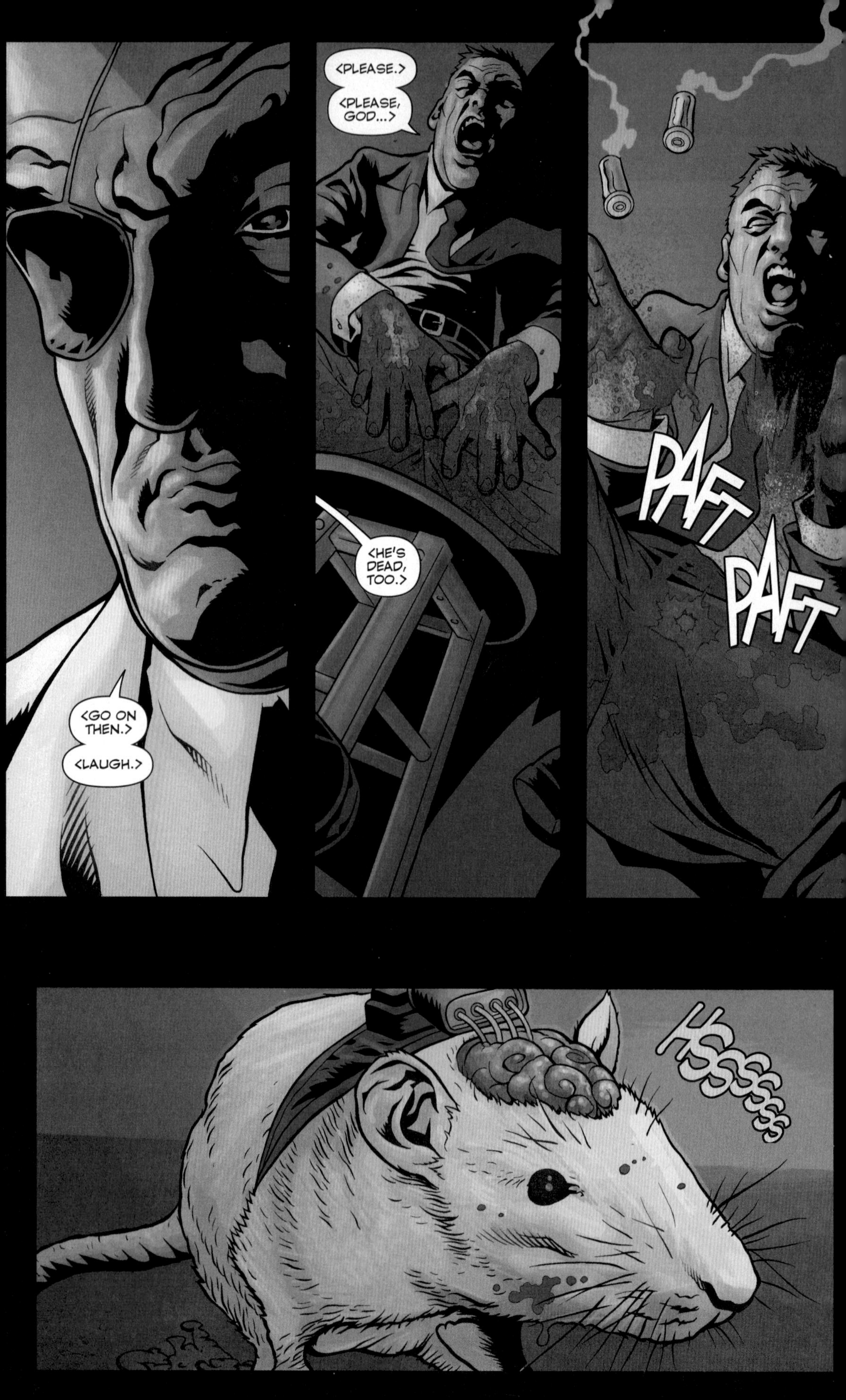
<GO ON THEN.>
<LAUGH.>
<PLEASE.>
<PLEASE, GOD...>
<HE'S DEAD, TOO.>
PAFT
PAFT
HSSSSSS

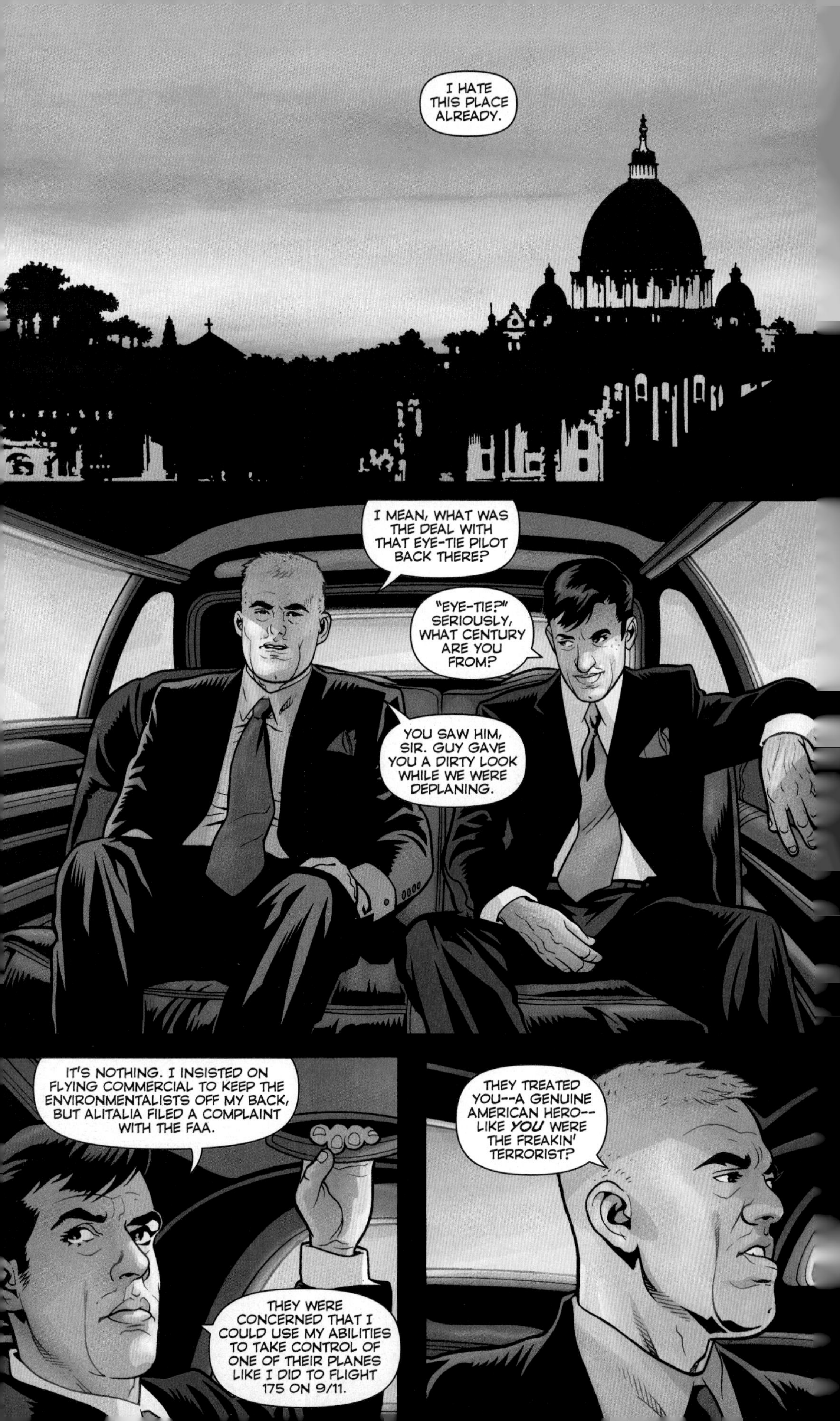
I HATE THIS PLACE ALREADY.
I MEAN, WHAT WAS THE DEAL WITH THAT EYE-TIE PILOT BACK THERE?
"EYE-TIE?" SERIOUSLY, WHAT CENTURY ARE YOU FROM?
YOU SAW HIM, SIR. GUY GAVE YOU A DIRTY LOOK WHILE WE WERE DEPLANING.
IT'S NOTHING. I INSISTED ON FLYING COMMERCIAL TO KEEP THE ENVIRONMENTALISTS OFF MY BACK, BUT ALITALIA FILED A COMPLAINT WITH THE FAA.
THEY WERE CONCERNED THAT I COULD USE MY ABILITIES TO TAKE CONTROL OF ONE OF THEIR PLANES LIKE I DID TO FLIGHT 175 ON 9/11.
THEY TREATED YOU--A GENUINE AMERICAN HERO--LIKE *YOU* WERE THE FREAKIN' TERRORIST?

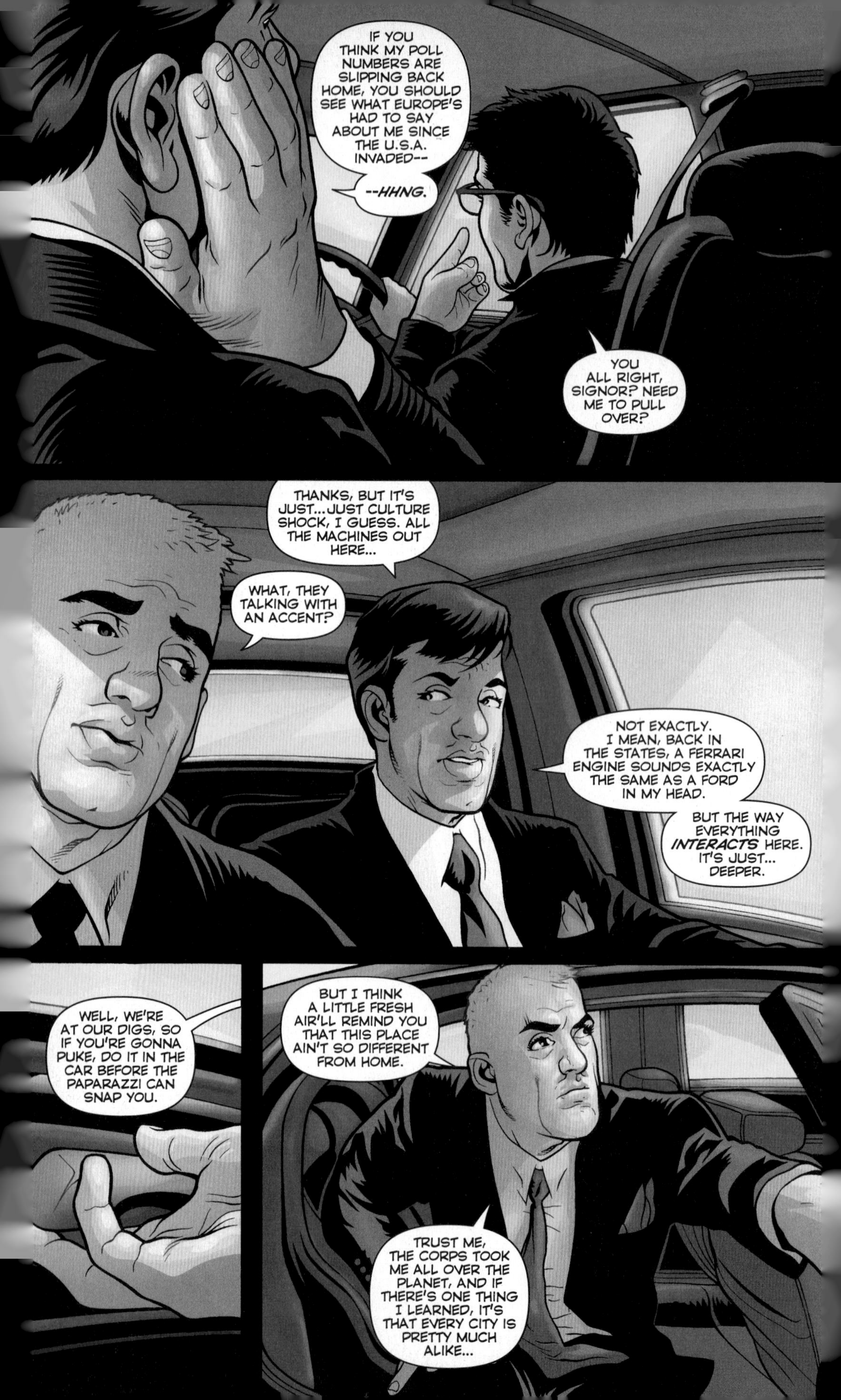
IF YOU THINK MY POLL NUMBERS ARE SLIPPING BACK HOME, YOU SHOULD SEE WHAT EUROPE'S HAD TO SAY ABOUT ME SINCE THE U.S.A. INVADED--
--HHNG.
YOU ALL RIGHT, SIGNOR? NEED ME TO PULL OVER?
THANKS, BUT IT'S JUST...JUST CULTURE SHOCK, I GUESS. ALL THE MACHINES OUT HERE...
WHAT, THEY TALKING WITH AN ACCENT?
NOT EXACTLY. I MEAN, BACK IN THE STATES, A FERRARI ENGINE SOUNDS EXACTLY THE SAME AS A FORD IN MY HEAD.
BUT THE WAY EVERYTHING *INTERACTS* HERE. IT'S JUST... DEEPER.
WELL, WE'RE AT OUR DIGS, SO IF YOU'RE GONNA PUKE, DO IT IN THE CAR BEFORE THE PAPARAZZI CAN SNAP YOU.
BUT I THINK A LITTLE FRESH AIR'LL REMIND YOU THAT THIS PLACE AIN'T SO DIFFERENT FROM HOME.
TRUST ME, THE CORPS TOOK ME ALL OVER THE PLANET, AND IF THERE'S ONE THING I LEARNED, IT'S THAT EVERY CITY IS PRETTY MUCH ALIKE...

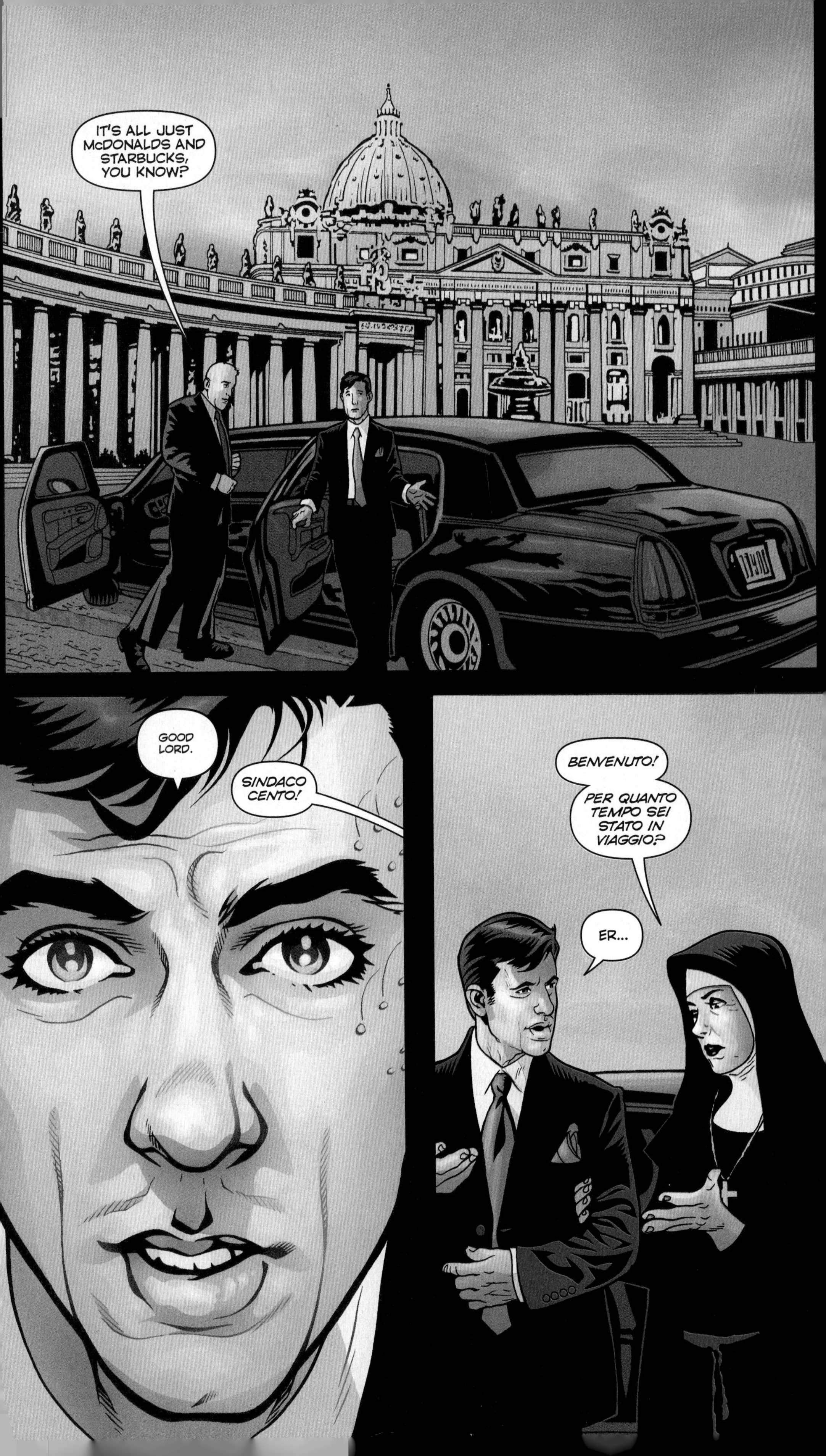
IT'S ALL JUST McDONALDS AND STARBUCKS, YOU KNOW?
GOOD LORD.
SINDACO CENTO!
BENVENUTO!
PER QUANTO TEMPO SEI STATO IN VIAGGIO?
ER...

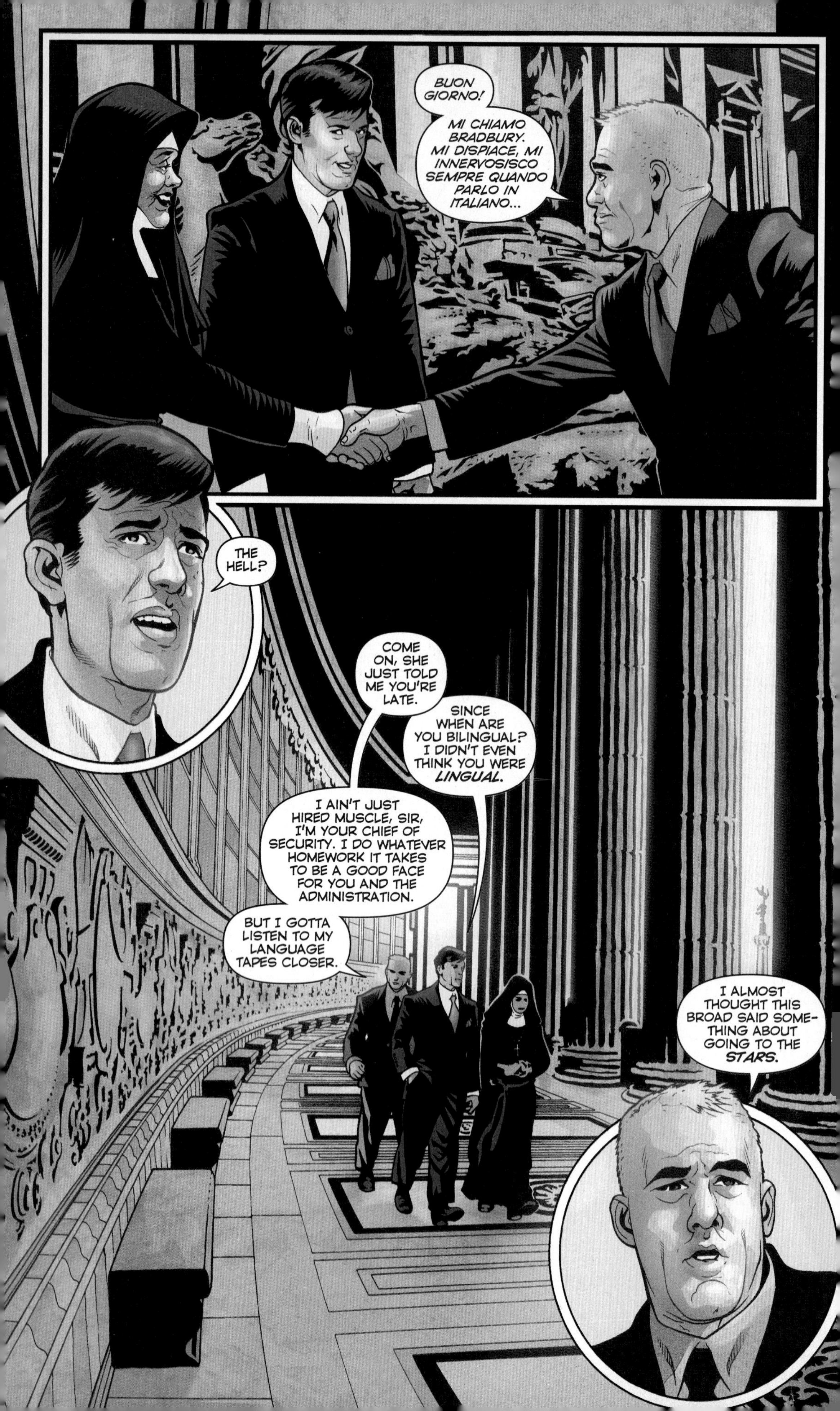
BUON GIORNO!
MI CHIAMO BRADBURY. MI DISPIACE, MI INNERVOSISCO SEMPRE QUANDO PARLO IN ITALIANO...
THE HELL?
COME ON, SHE JUST TOLD ME YOU'RE LATE.
SINCE WHEN ARE YOU BILINGUAL? I DIDN'T EVEN THINK YOU WERE LINGUAL.
I AIN'T JUST HIRED MUSCLE, SIR, I'M YOUR CHIEF OF SECURITY. I DO WHATEVER HOMEWORK IT TAKES TO BE A GOOD FACE FOR YOU AND THE ADMINISTRATION.
BUT I GOTTA LISTEN TO MY LANGUAGE TAPES CLOSER.
I ALMOST THOUGHT THIS BROAD SAID SOMETHING ABOUT GOING TO THE STARS.

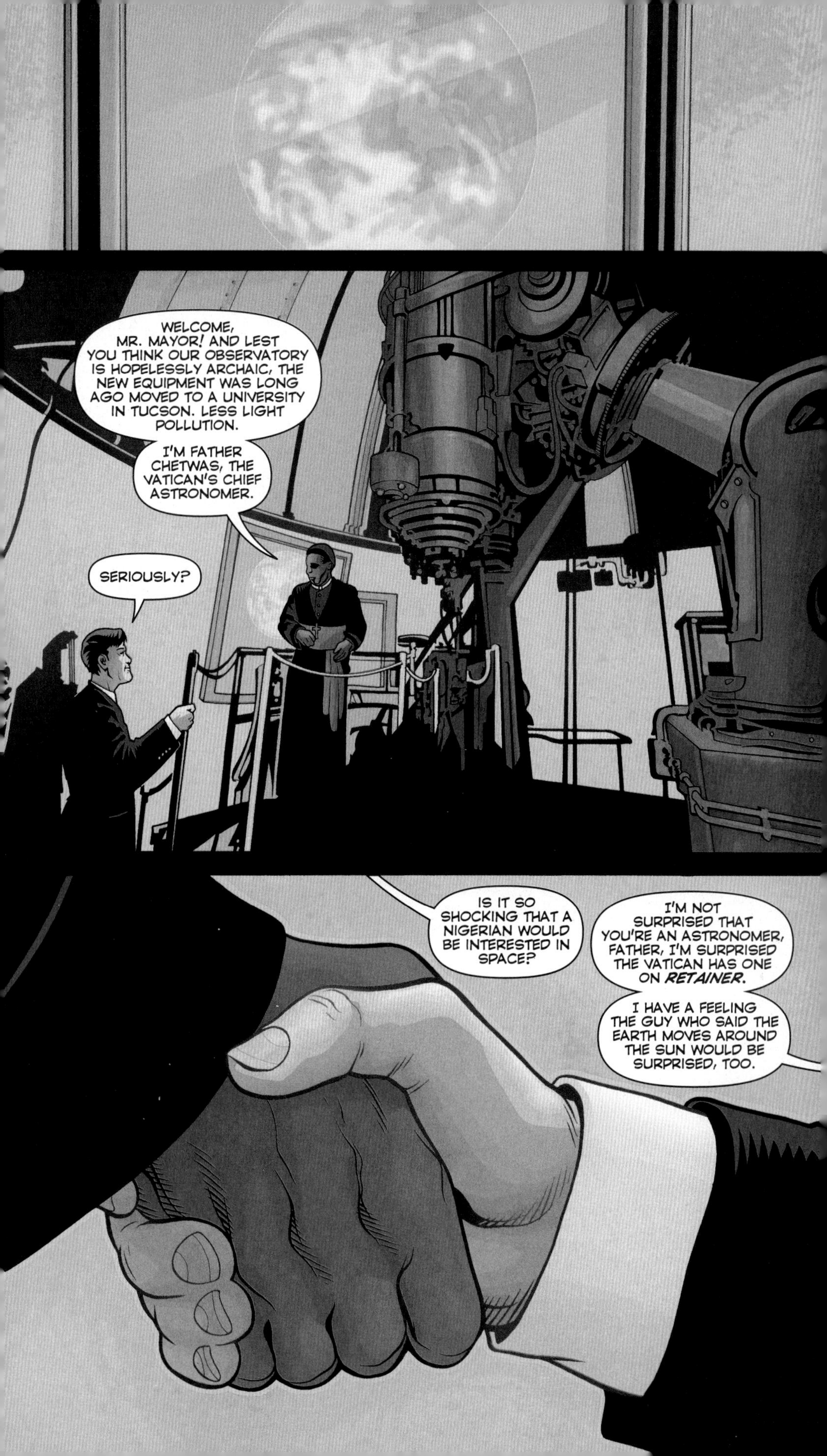

WELCOME, MR. MAYOR! AND LEST YOU THINK OUR OBSERVATORY IS HOPELESSLY ARCHAIC, THE NEW EQUIPMENT WAS LONG AGO MOVED TO A UNIVERSITY IN TUCSON. LESS LIGHT POLLUTION.
I'M FATHER CHETWAS, THE VATICAN'S CHIEF ASTRONOMER.
SERIOUSLY?
IS IT SO SHOCKING THAT A NIGERIAN WOULD BE INTERESTED IN SPACE?
I'M NOT SURPRISED THAT YOU'RE AN ASTRONOMER, FATHER, I'M SURPRISED THE VATICAN HAS ONE ON *RETAINER*.
I HAVE A FEELING THE GUY WHO SAID THE EARTH MOVES AROUND THE SUN WOULD BE SURPRISED, TOO.

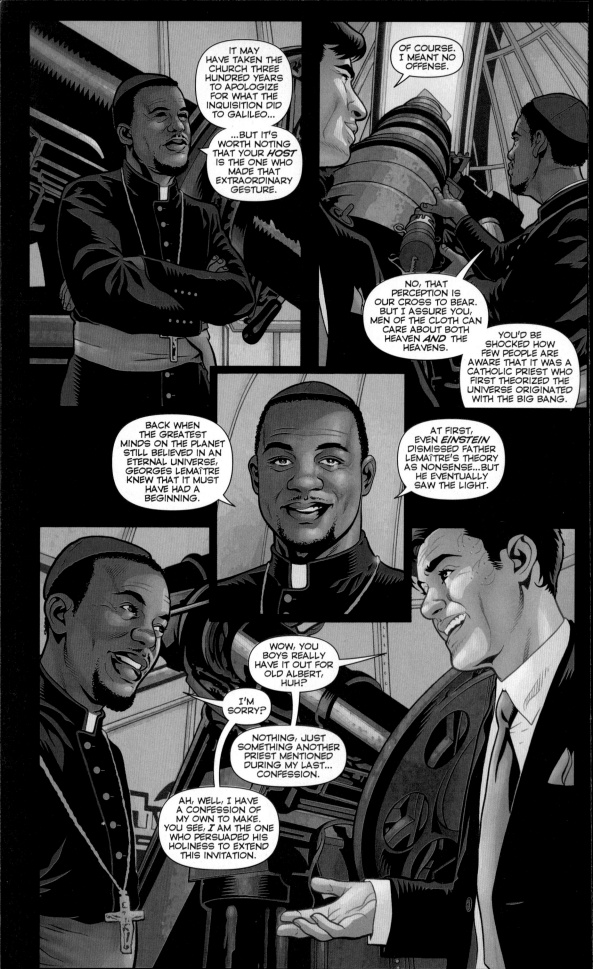

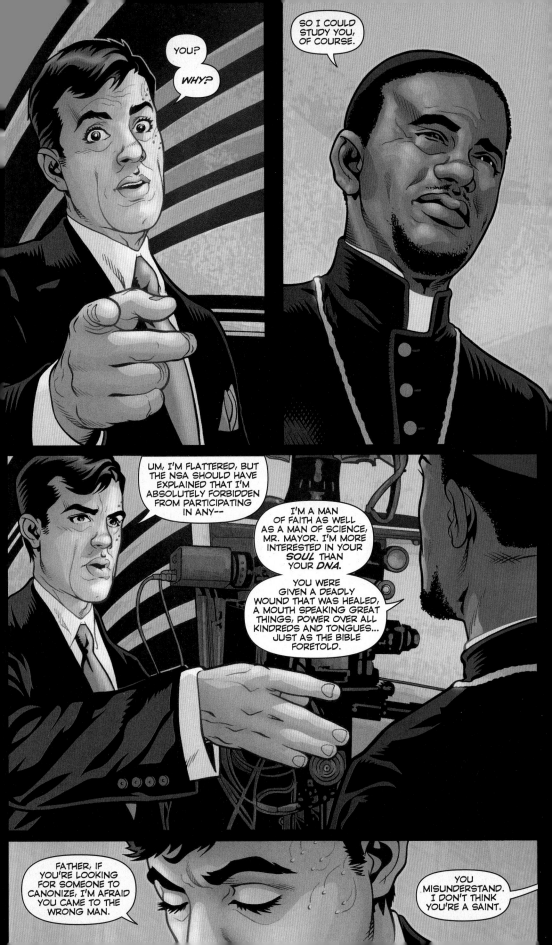

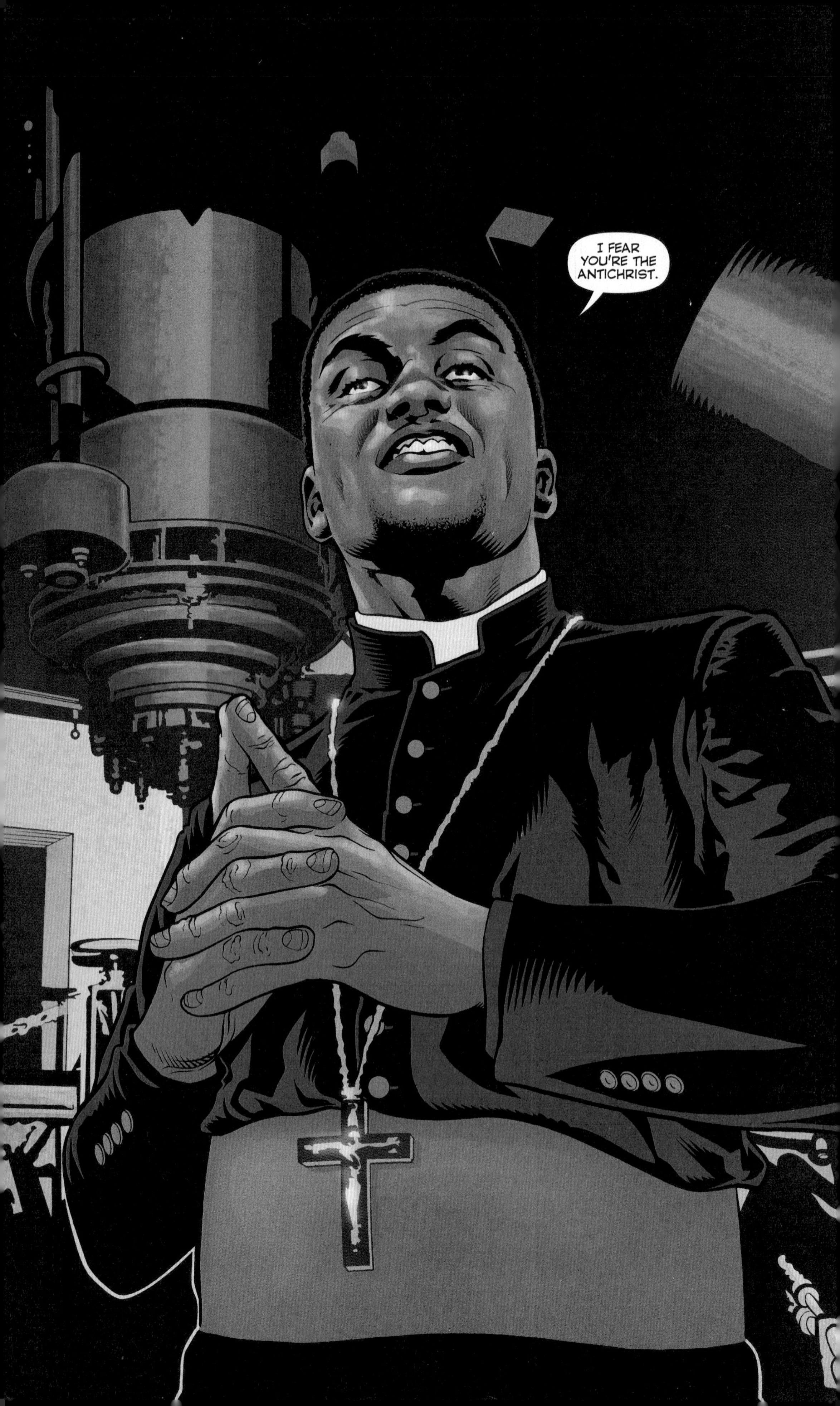
I FEAR YOU'RE THE ANTICHRIST.

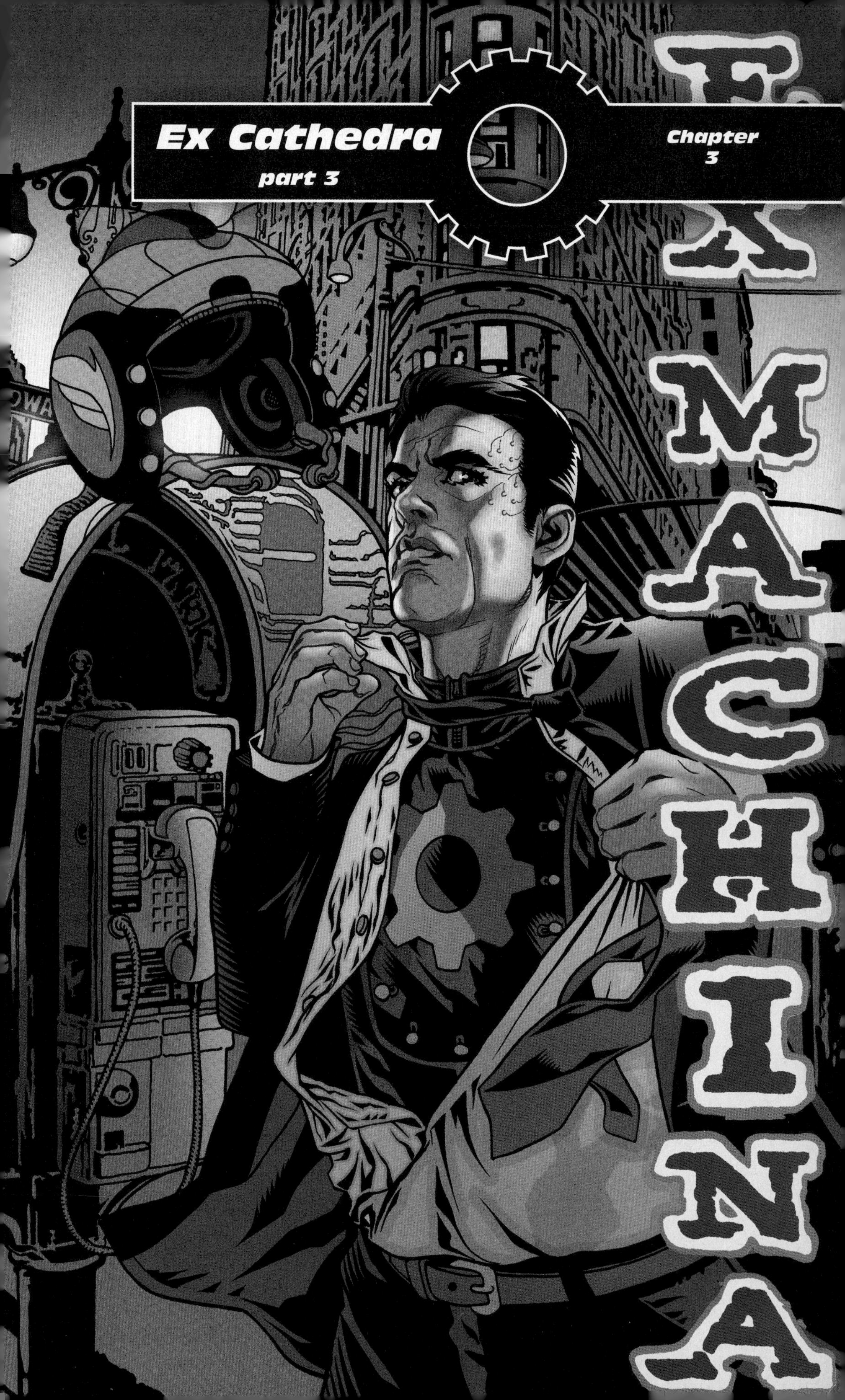
Ex Cathedra
part 3
Chapter
3
EX MACHINA

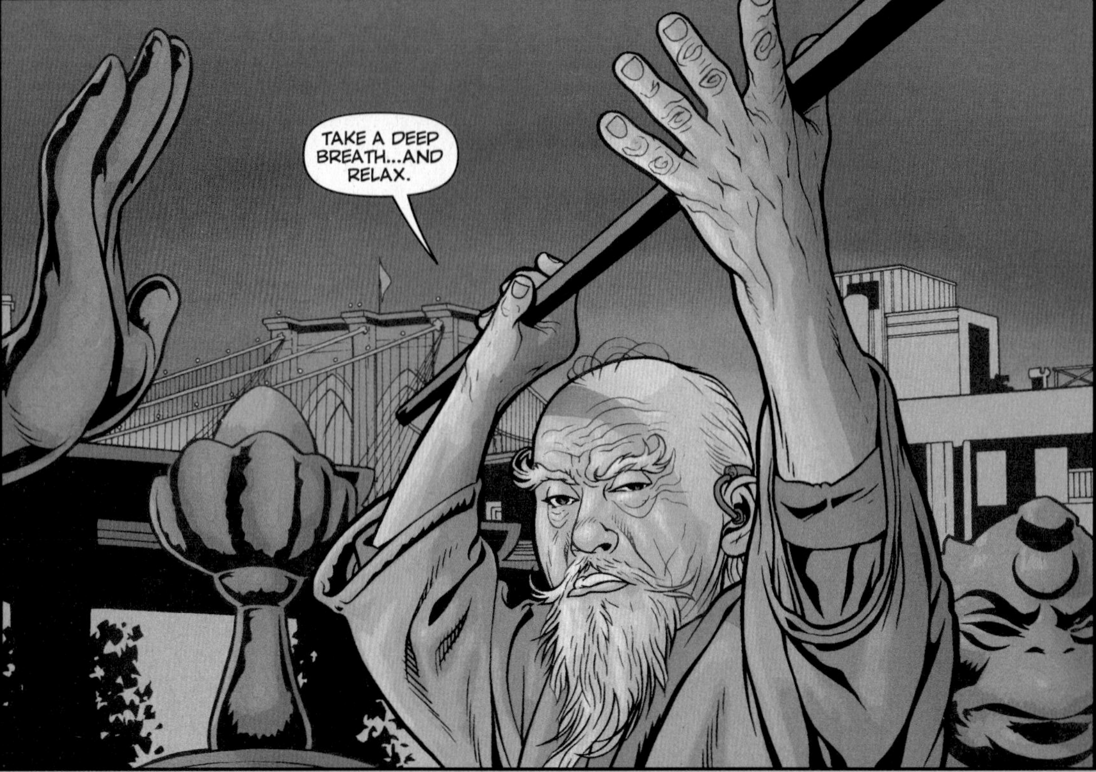
TAKE A DEEP BREATH...AND RELAX.

TUESDAY, MAY 29, 2001

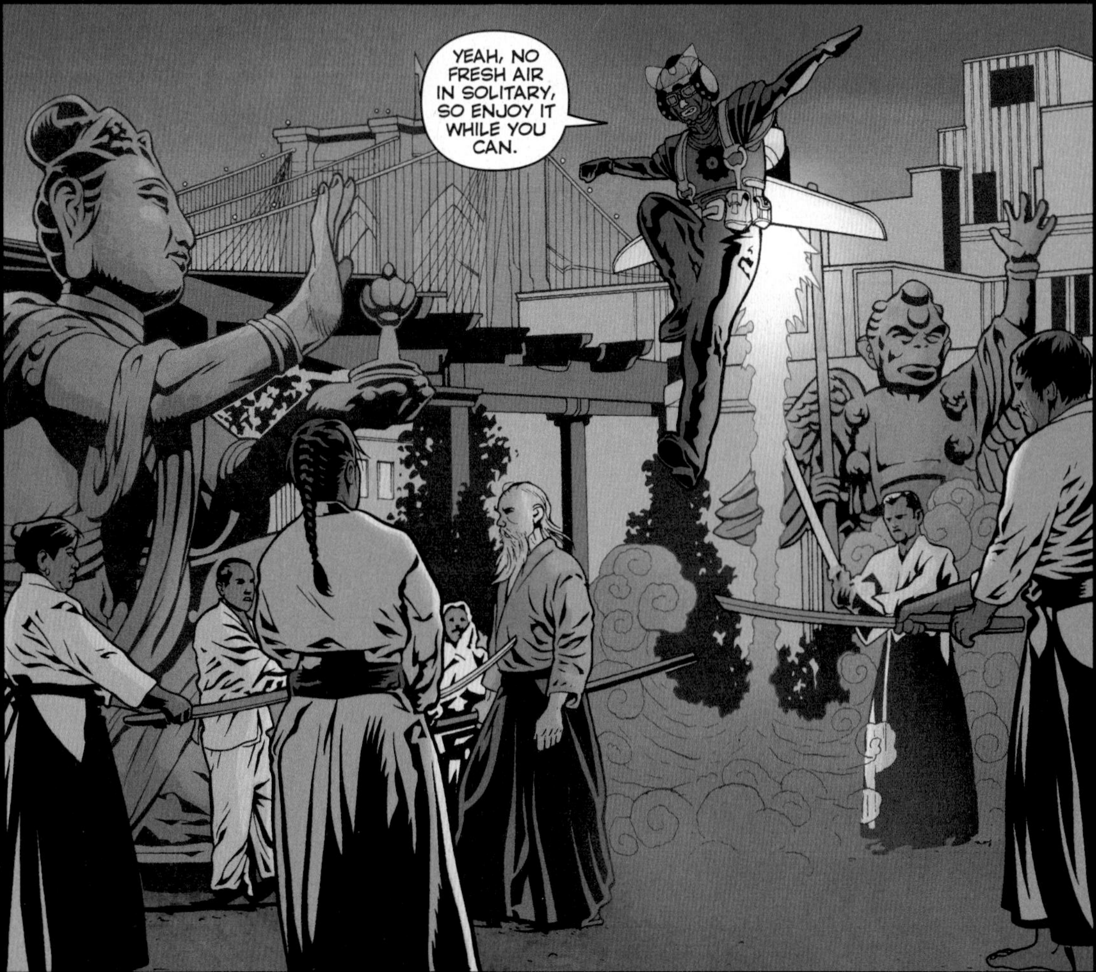
YEAH, NO FRESH AIR IN SOLITARY, SO ENJOY IT WHILE YOU CAN.

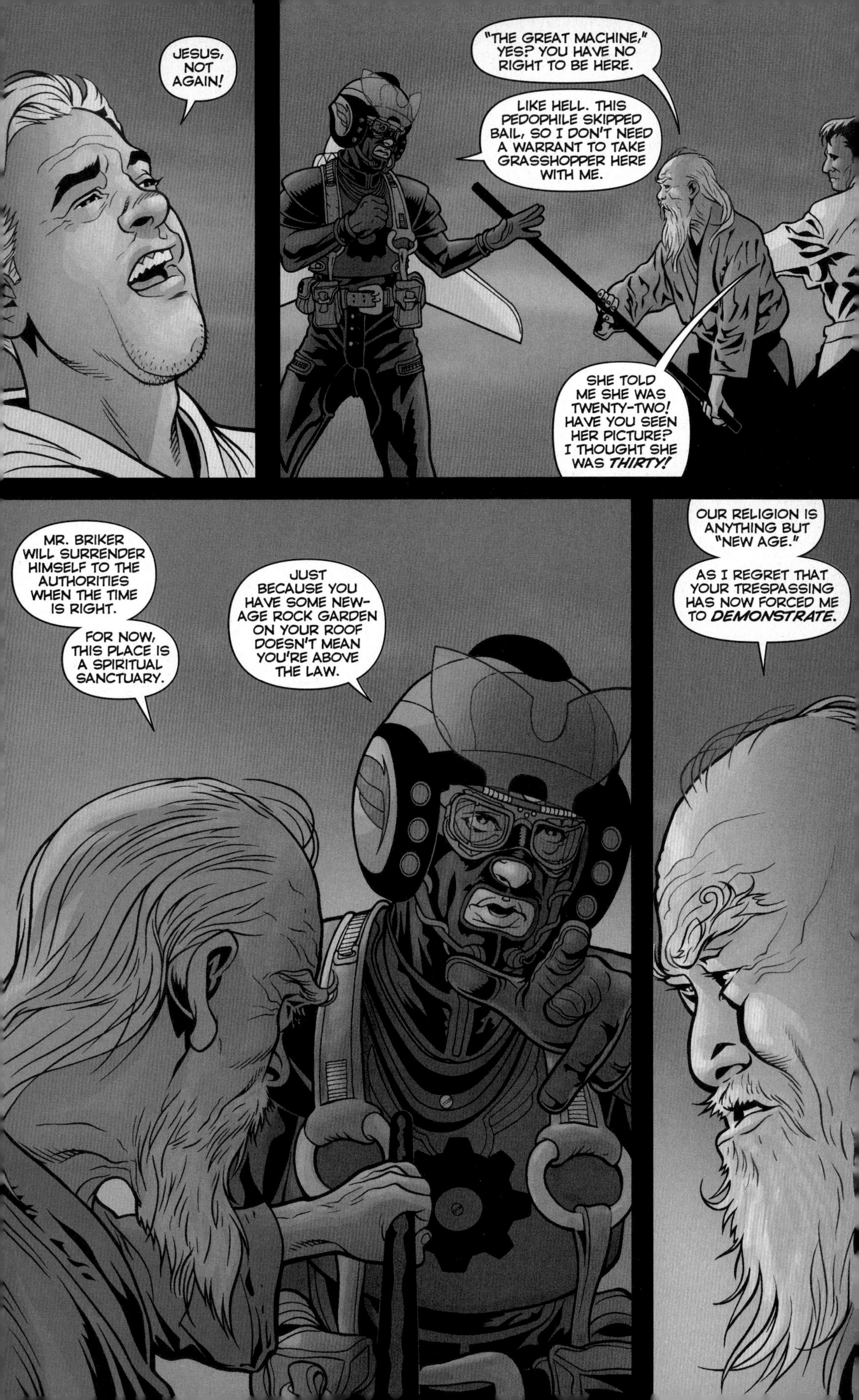
JESUS, NOT AGAIN!
"THE GREAT MACHINE," YES? YOU HAVE NO RIGHT TO BE HERE.
LIKE HELL. THIS PEDOPHILE SKIPPED BAIL, SO I DON'T NEED A WARRANT TO TAKE GRASSHOPPER HERE WITH ME.
SHE TOLD ME SHE WAS TWENTY-TWO! HAVE YOU SEEN HER PICTURE? I THOUGHT SHE WAS THIRTY!
MR. BRIKER WILL SURRENDER HIMSELF TO THE AUTHORITIES WHEN THE TIME IS RIGHT.
FOR NOW, THIS PLACE IS A SPIRITUAL SANCTUARY.
JUST BECAUSE YOU HAVE SOME NEW-AGE ROCK GARDEN ON YOUR ROOF DOESN'T MEAN YOU'RE ABOVE THE LAW.
OUR RELIGION IS ANYTHING BUT "NEW AGE."
AS I REGRET THAT YOUR TRESPASSING HAS NOW FORCED ME TO DEMONSTRATE.

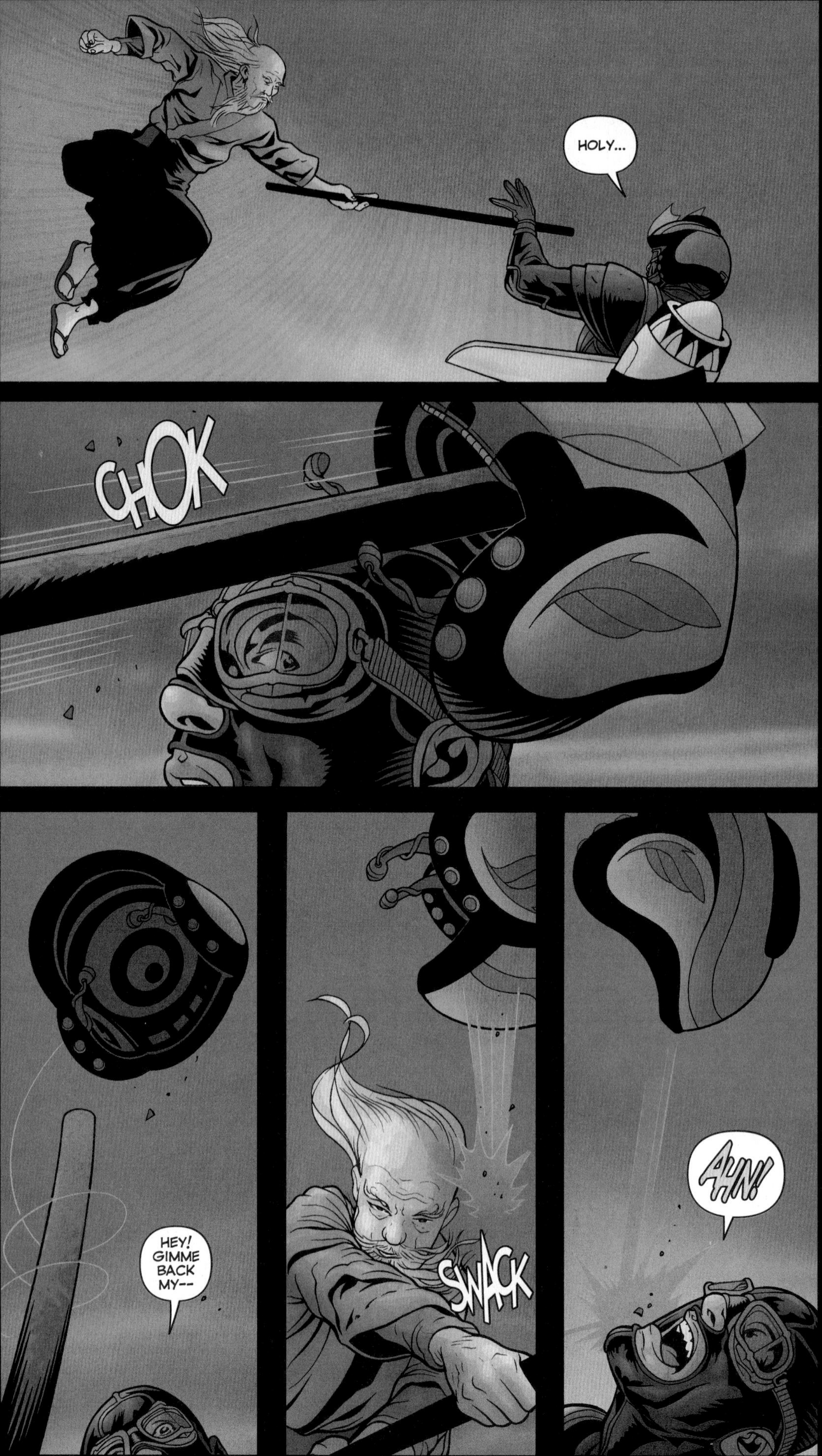
HOLY...
CHOK
HEY! GIMME BACK MY--
SWACK
AHN!

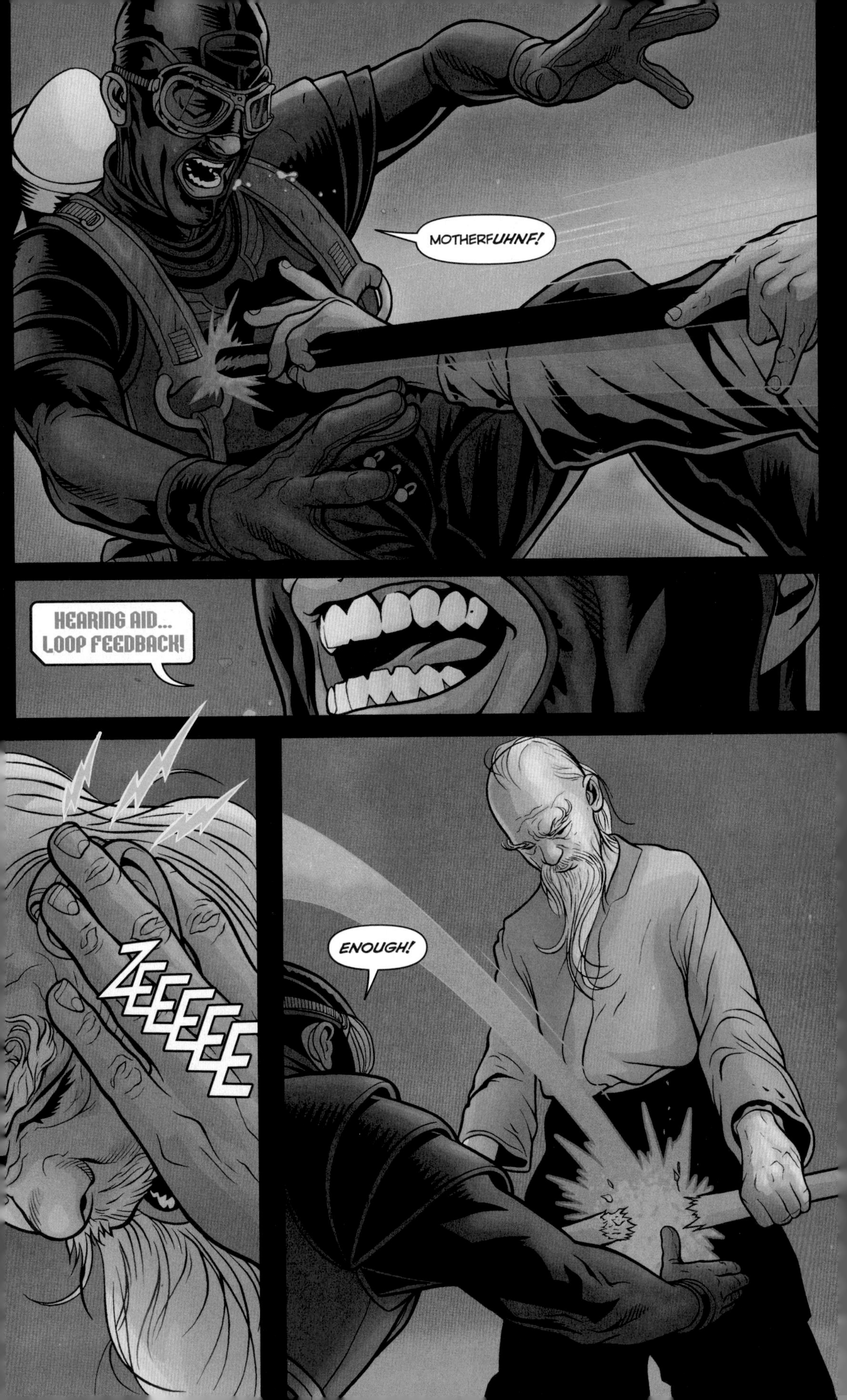
MOTHERFUHNF!
HEARING AID...
LOOP FEEDBACK!
ZEEEEEE
ENOUGH!

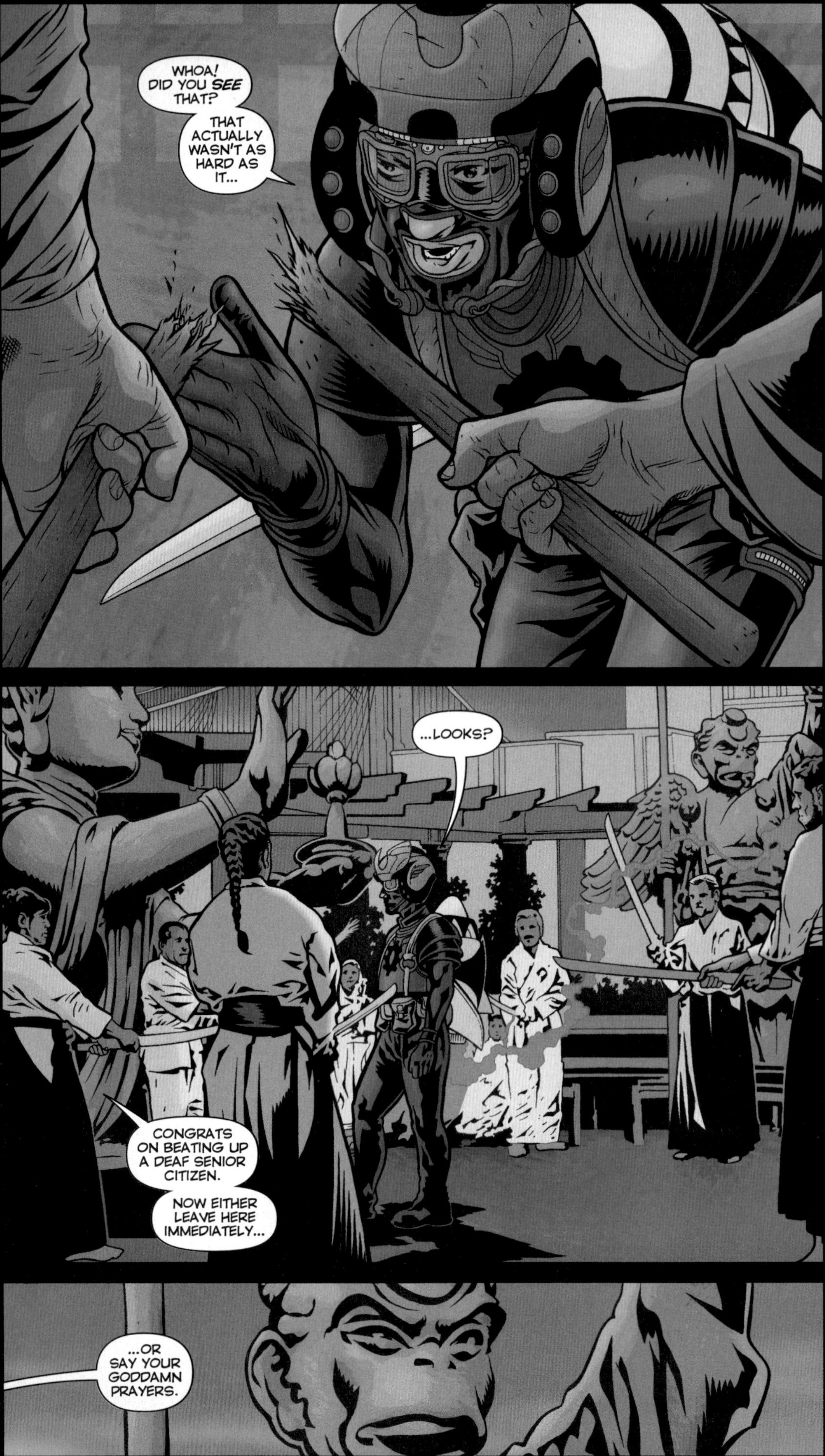
WHOA! DID YOU SEE THAT?
THAT ACTUALLY WASN'T AS HARD AS IT...
...LOOKS?
CONGRATS ON BEATING UP A DEAF SENIOR CITIZEN.
NOW EITHER LEAVE HERE IMMEDIATELY...
...OR SAY YOUR GODDAMN PRAYERS.

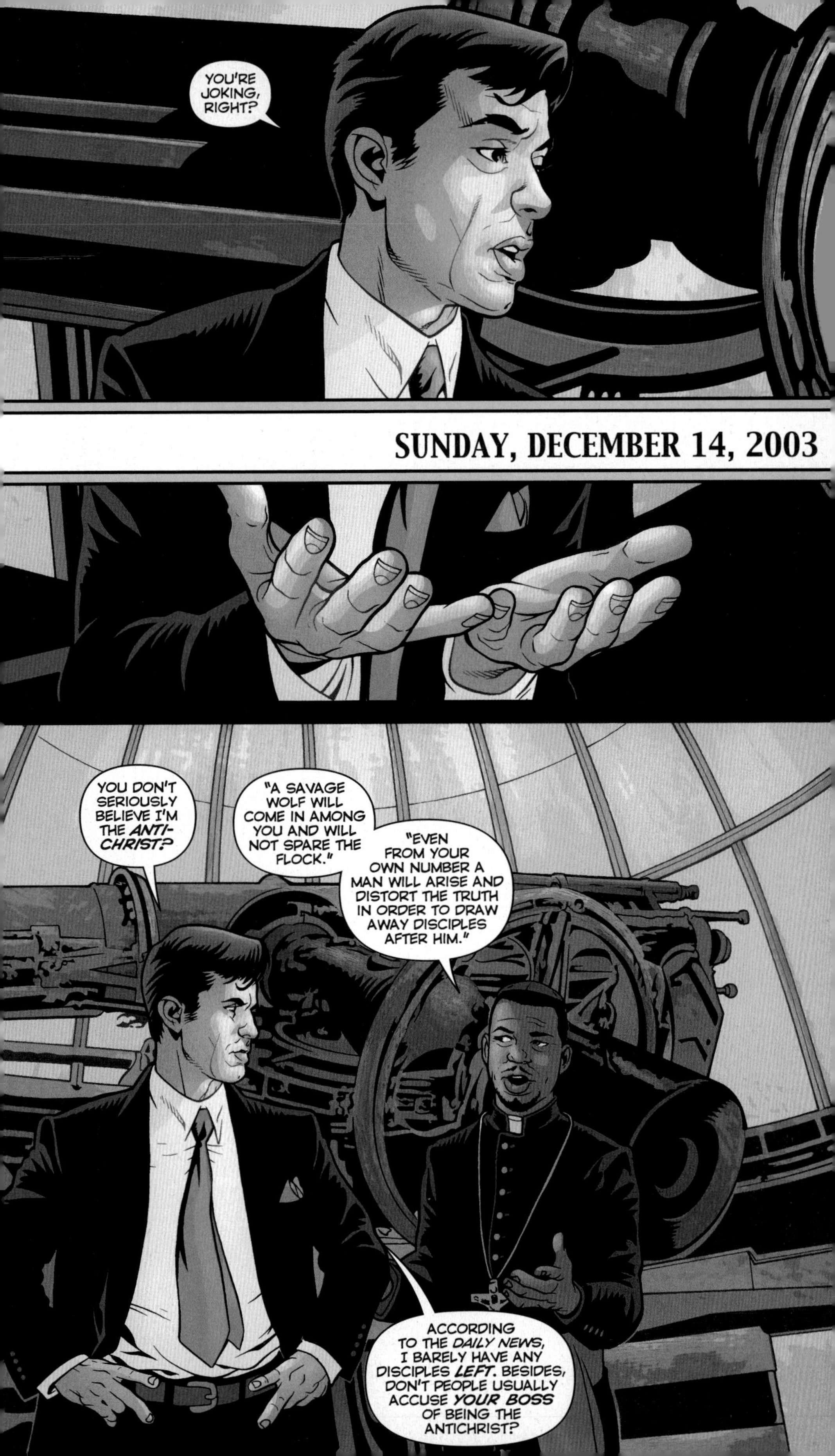

YOU'RE JOKING, RIGHT?
SUNDAY, DECEMBER 14, 2003
YOU DON'T SERIOUSLY BELIEVE I'M THE *ANTI-CHRIST?*
"A SAVAGE WOLF WILL COME IN AMONG YOU AND WILL NOT SPARE THE FLOCK."
"EVEN FROM YOUR OWN NUMBER A MAN WILL ARISE AND DISTORT THE TRUTH IN ORDER TO DRAW AWAY DISCIPLES AFTER HIM."
ACCORDING TO THE *DAILY NEWS*, I BARELY HAVE ANY DISCIPLES *LEFT*. BESIDES, DON'T PEOPLE USUALLY ACCUSE ***YOUR BOSS*** OF BEING THE ANTICHRIST?

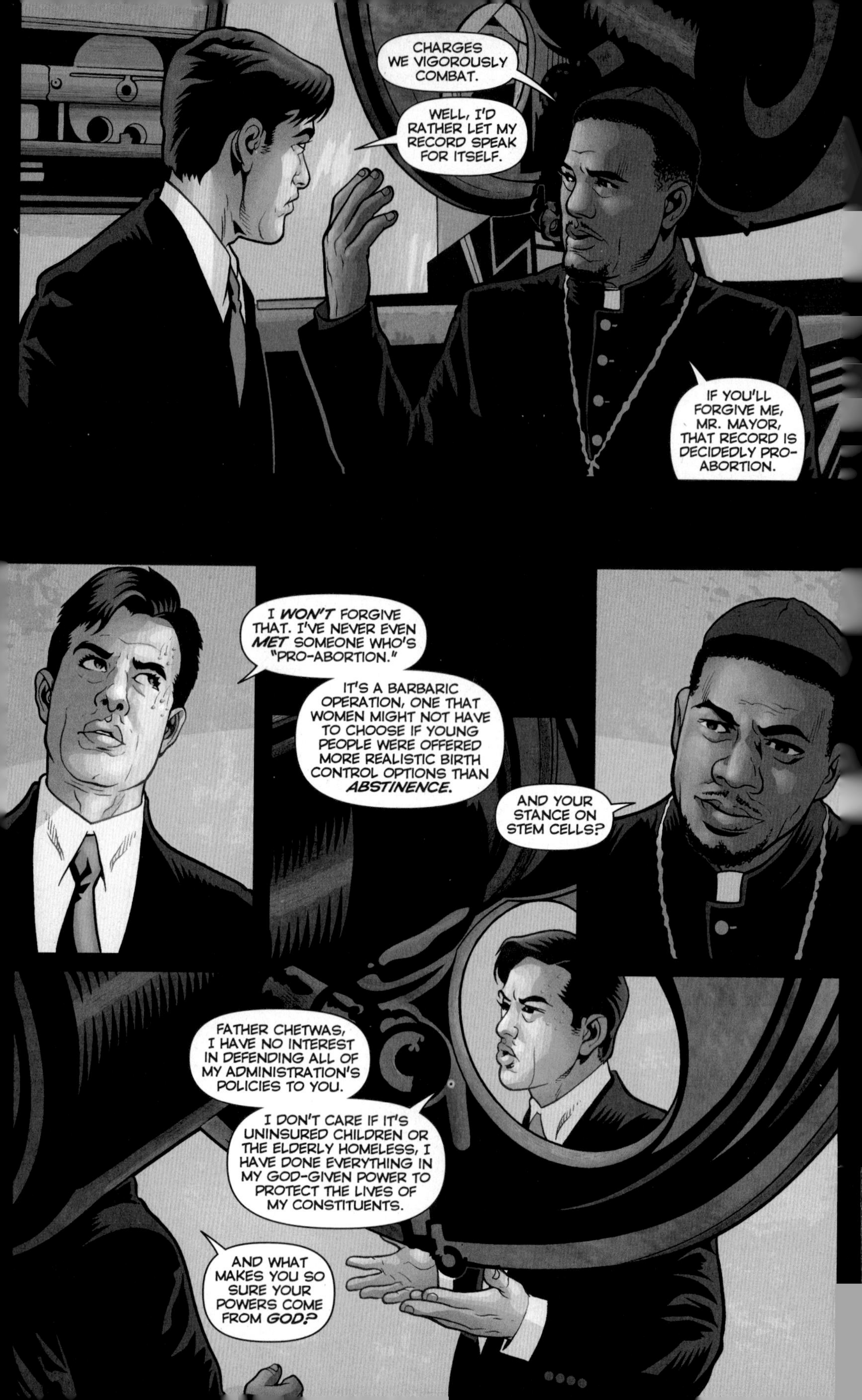
CHARGES WE VIGOROUSLY COMBAT.
WELL, I'D RATHER LET MY RECORD SPEAK FOR ITSELF.
IF YOU'LL FORGIVE ME, MR. MAYOR, THAT RECORD IS DECIDEDLY PRO-ABORTION.
I *WON'T* FORGIVE THAT. I'VE NEVER EVEN *MET* SOMEONE WHO'S "PRO-ABORTION."
IT'S A BARBARIC OPERATION, ONE THAT WOMEN MIGHT NOT HAVE TO CHOOSE IF YOUNG PEOPLE WERE OFFERED MORE REALISTIC BIRTH CONTROL OPTIONS THAN *ABSTINENCE*.
AND YOUR STANCE ON STEM CELLS?
FATHER CHETWAS, I HAVE NO INTEREST IN DEFENDING ALL OF MY ADMINISTRATION'S POLICIES TO YOU.
I DON'T CARE IF IT'S UNINSURED CHILDREN OR THE ELDERLY HOMELESS, I HAVE DONE EVERYTHING IN MY GOD-GIVEN POWER TO PROTECT THE LIVES OF MY CONSTITUENTS.
AND WHAT MAKES YOU SO SURE YOUR POWERS COME FROM *GOD*?

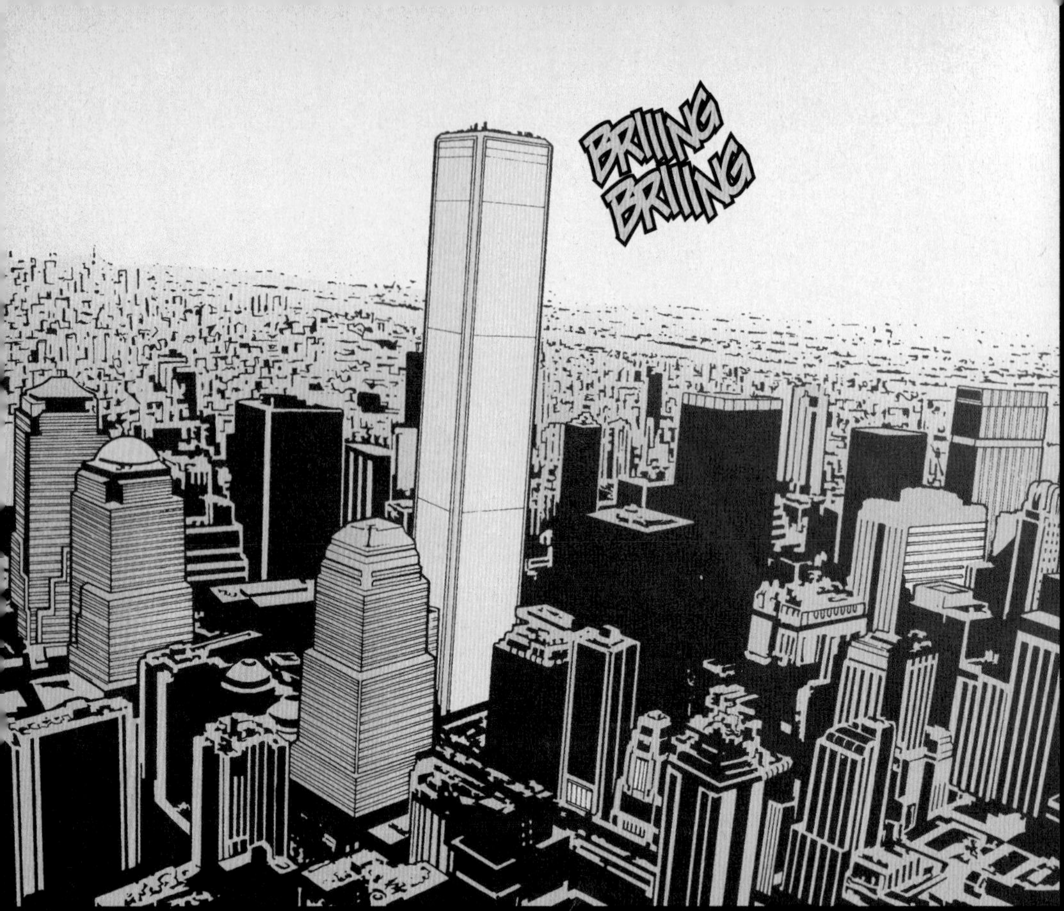
BRIIING BRIIING

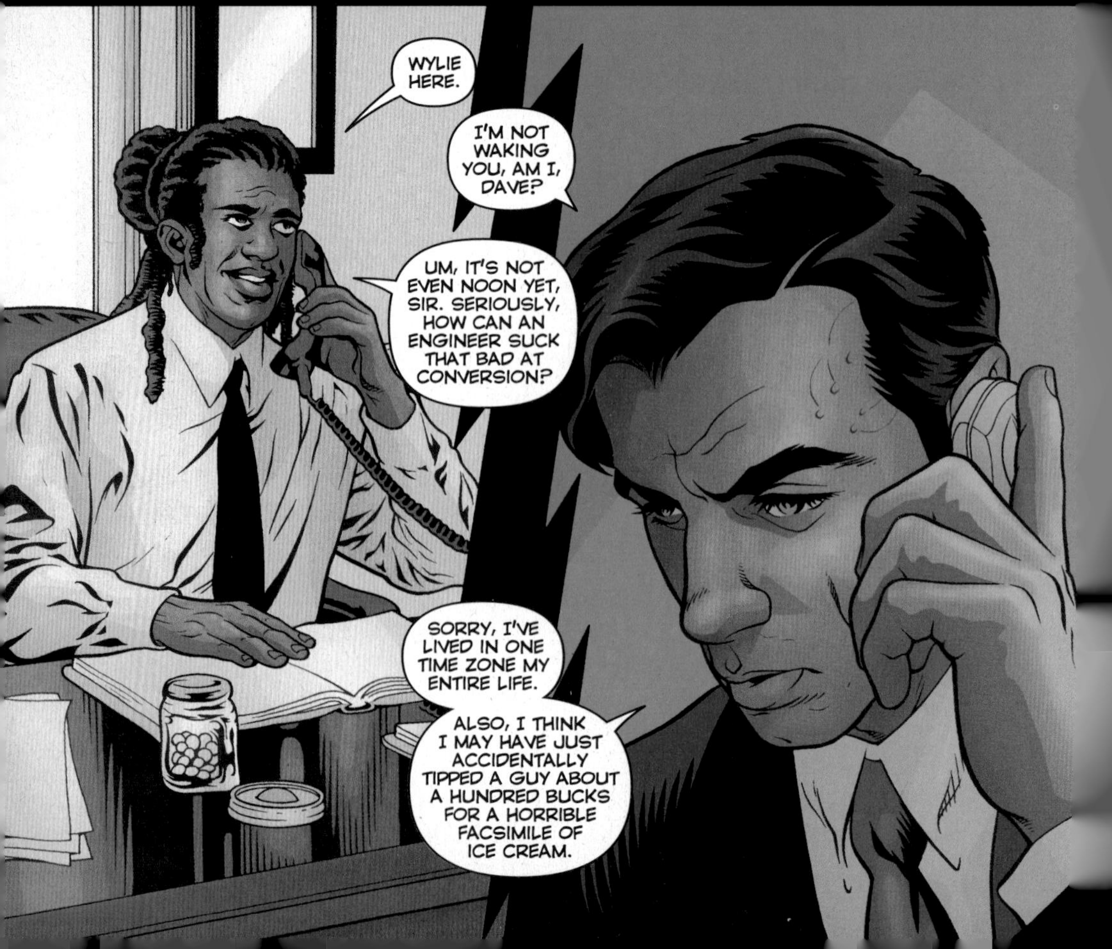
WYLIE HERE.
I'M NOT WAKING YOU, AM I, DAVE?
UM, IT'S NOT EVEN NOON YET, SIR. SERIOUSLY, HOW CAN AN ENGINEER SUCK THAT BAD AT CONVERSION?
SORRY, I'VE LIVED IN ONE TIME ZONE MY ENTIRE LIFE.
ALSO, I THINK I MAY HAVE JUST ACCIDENTALLY TIPPED A GUY ABOUT A HUNDRED BUCKS FOR A HORRIBLE FACSIMILE OF ICE CREAM.

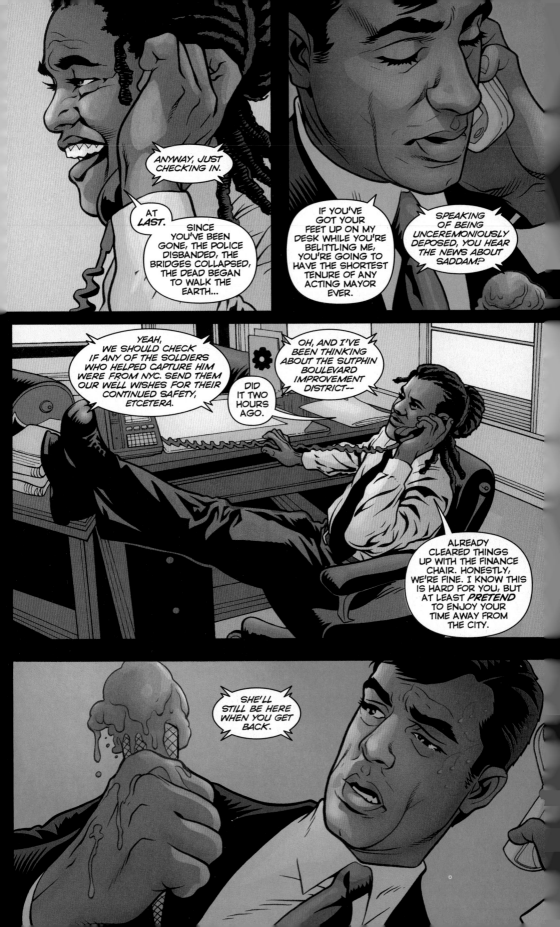

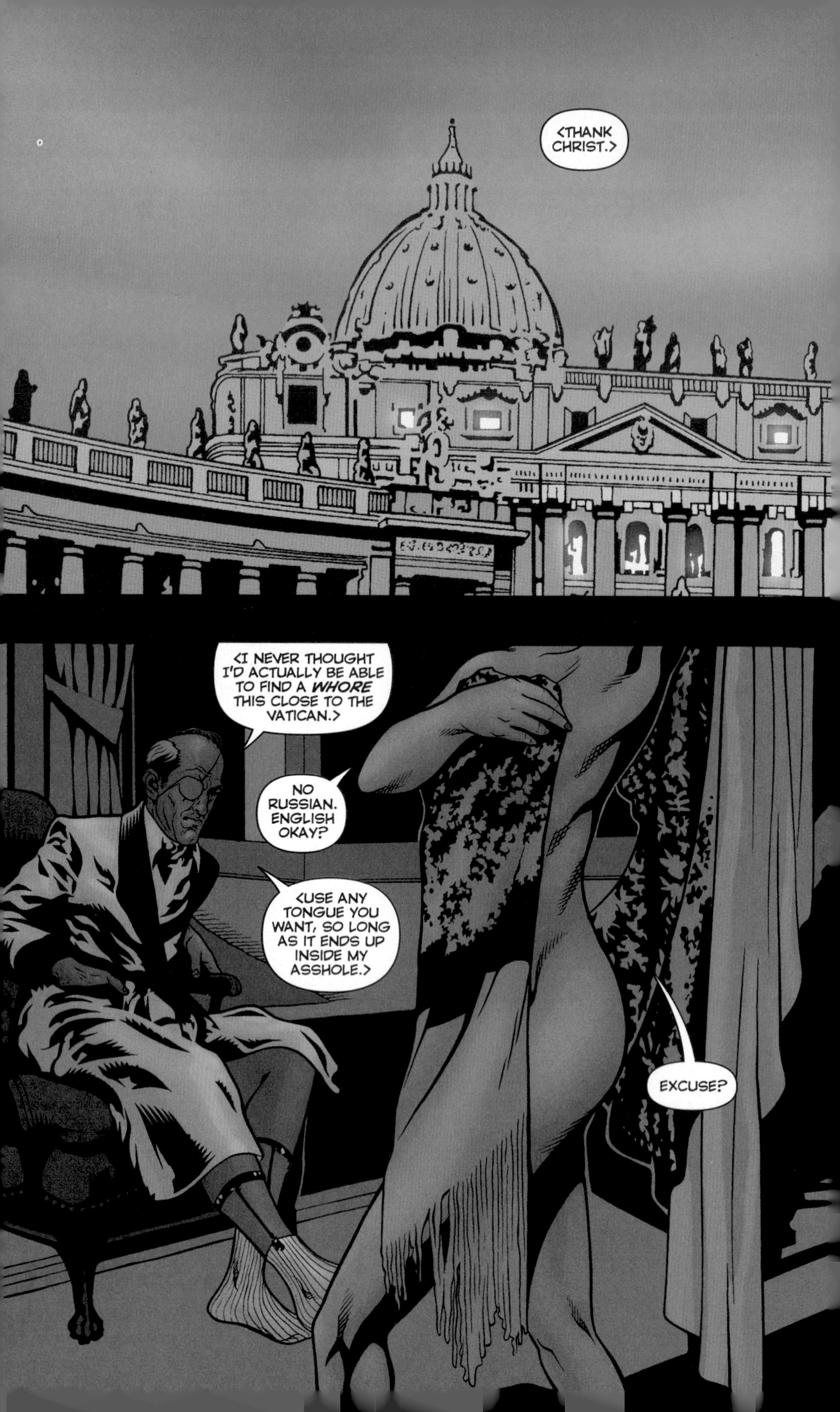
<THANK CHRIST.>
<I NEVER THOUGHT I'D ACTUALLY BE ABLE TO FIND A *WHORE* THIS CLOSE TO THE VATICAN.>
NO RUSSIAN. ENGLISH OKAY?
<USE ANY TONGUE YOU WANT, SO LONG AS IT ENDS UP INSIDE MY ASSHOLE.>
EXCUSE?

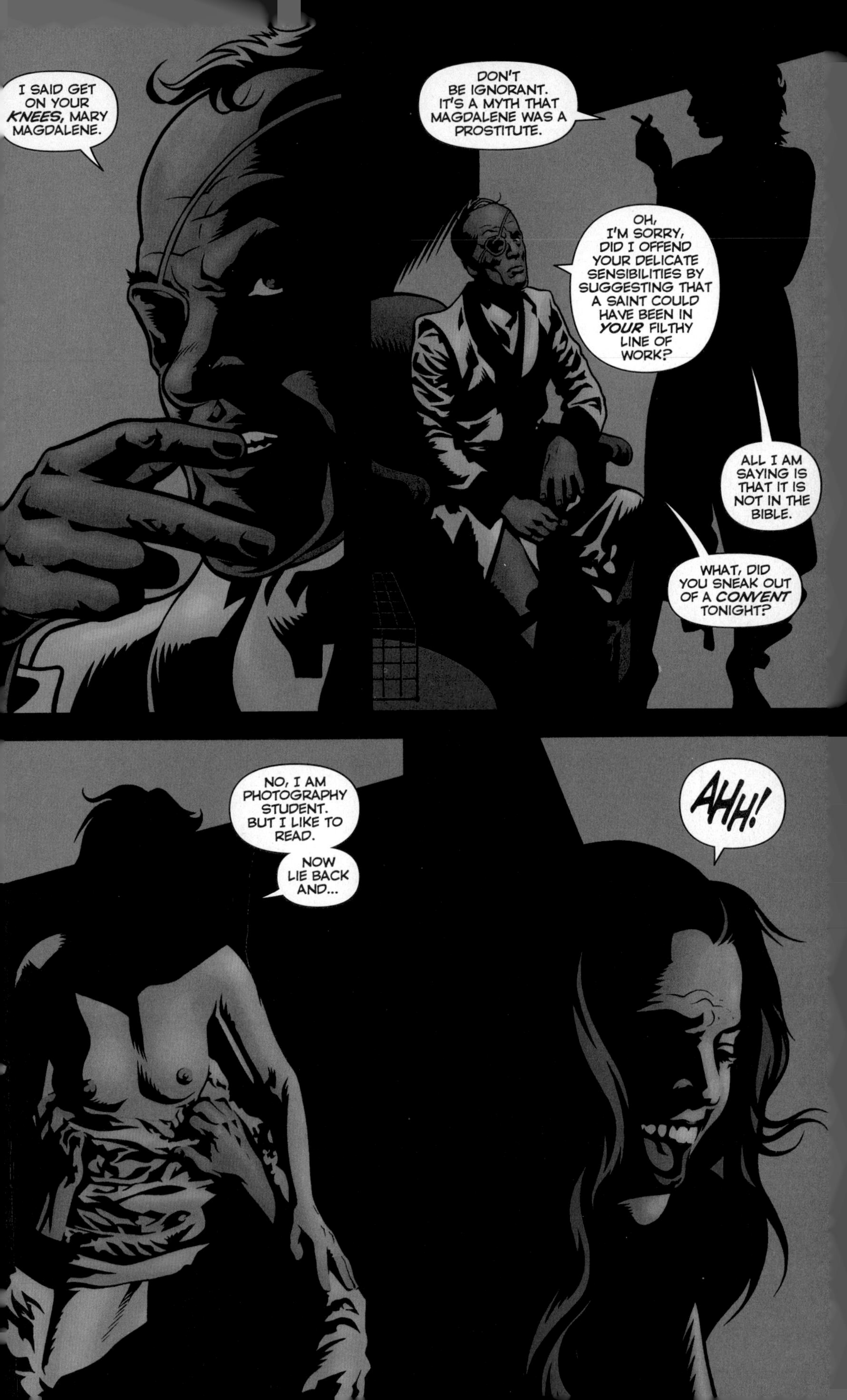
I SAID GET ON YOUR *KNEES,* MARY MAGDALENE.
DON'T BE IGNORANT. IT'S A MYTH THAT MAGDALENE WAS A PROSTITUTE.
OH, I'M SORRY, DID I OFFEND YOUR DELICATE SENSIBILITIES BY SUGGESTING THAT A SAINT COULD HAVE BEEN IN *YOUR* FILTHY LINE OF WORK?
ALL I AM SAYING IS THAT IT IS NOT IN THE BIBLE.
WHAT, DID YOU SNEAK OUT OF A *CONVENT* TONIGHT?
NO, I AM PHOTOGRAPHY STUDENT. BUT I LIKE TO READ.
NOW LIE BACK AND...
AHH!

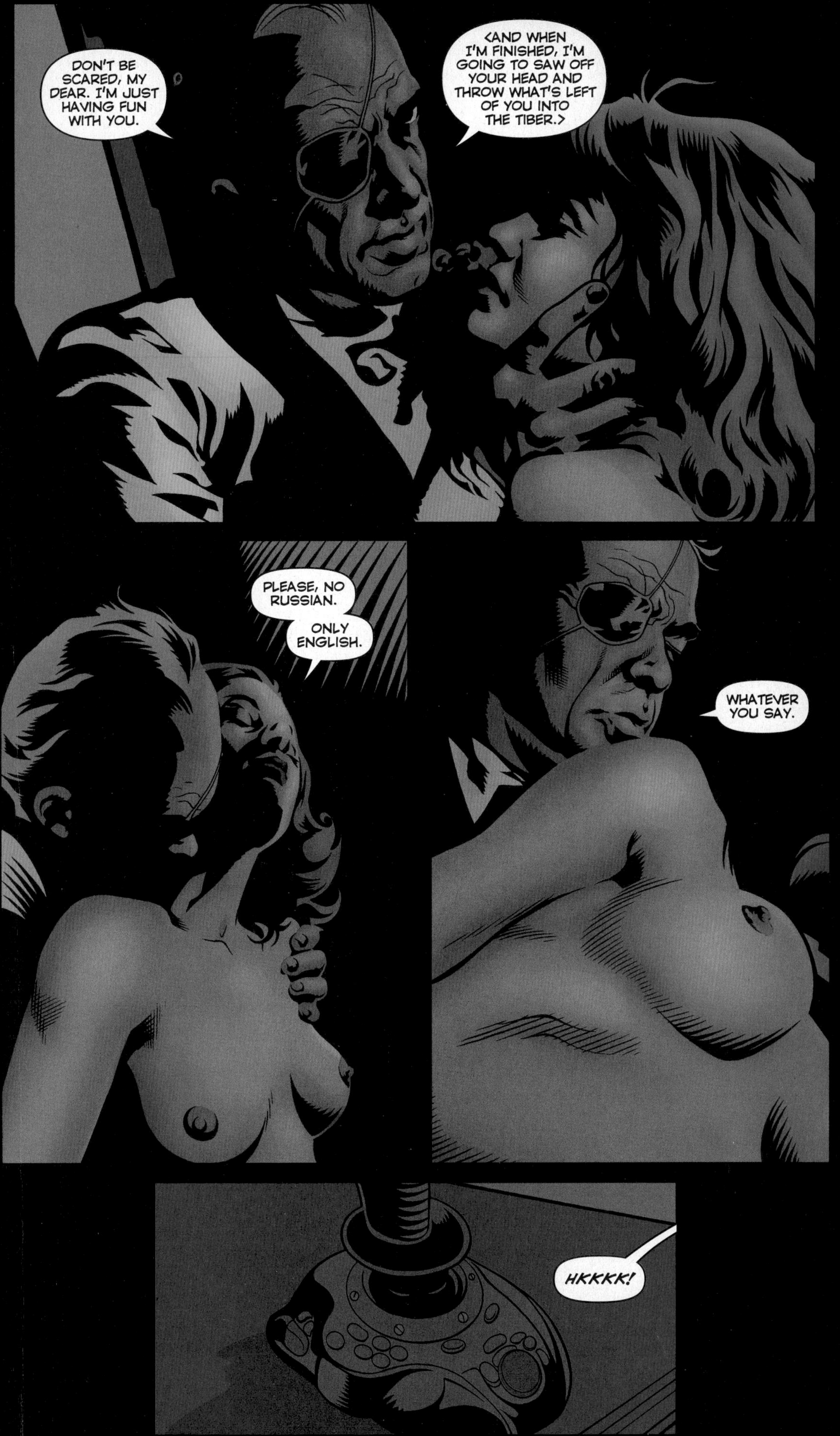
DON'T BE SCARED, MY DEAR. I'M JUST HAVING FUN WITH YOU.
<AND WHEN I'M FINISHED, I'M GOING TO SAW OFF YOUR HEAD AND THROW WHAT'S LEFT OF YOU INTO THE TIBER.>
PLEASE, NO RUSSIAN.
ONLY ENGLISH.
WHATEVER YOU SAY.
HKKKK!

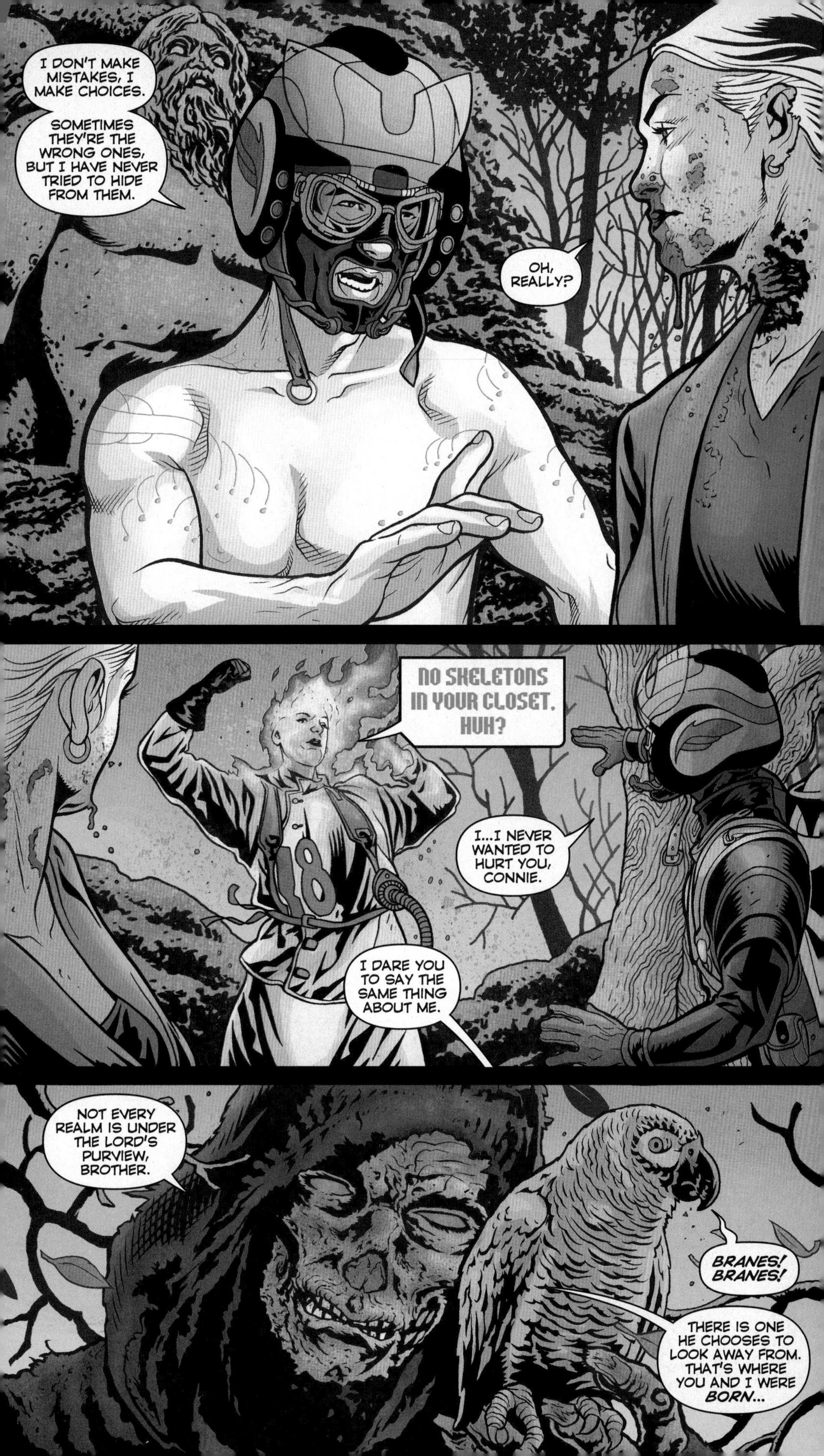
I DON'T MAKE MISTAKES, I MAKE CHOICES.
SOMETIMES THEY'RE THE WRONG ONES, BUT I HAVE NEVER TRIED TO HIDE FROM THEM.
OH, REALLY?
NO SKELETONS IN YOUR CLOSET, HUH?
I...I NEVER WANTED TO HURT YOU, CONNIE.
I DARE YOU TO SAY THE SAME THING ABOUT ME.
NOT EVERY REALM IS UNDER THE LORD'S PURVIEW, BROTHER.
BRANES! BRANES!
THERE IS ONE HE CHOOSES TO LOOK AWAY FROM. THAT'S WHERE YOU AND I WERE *BORN*...

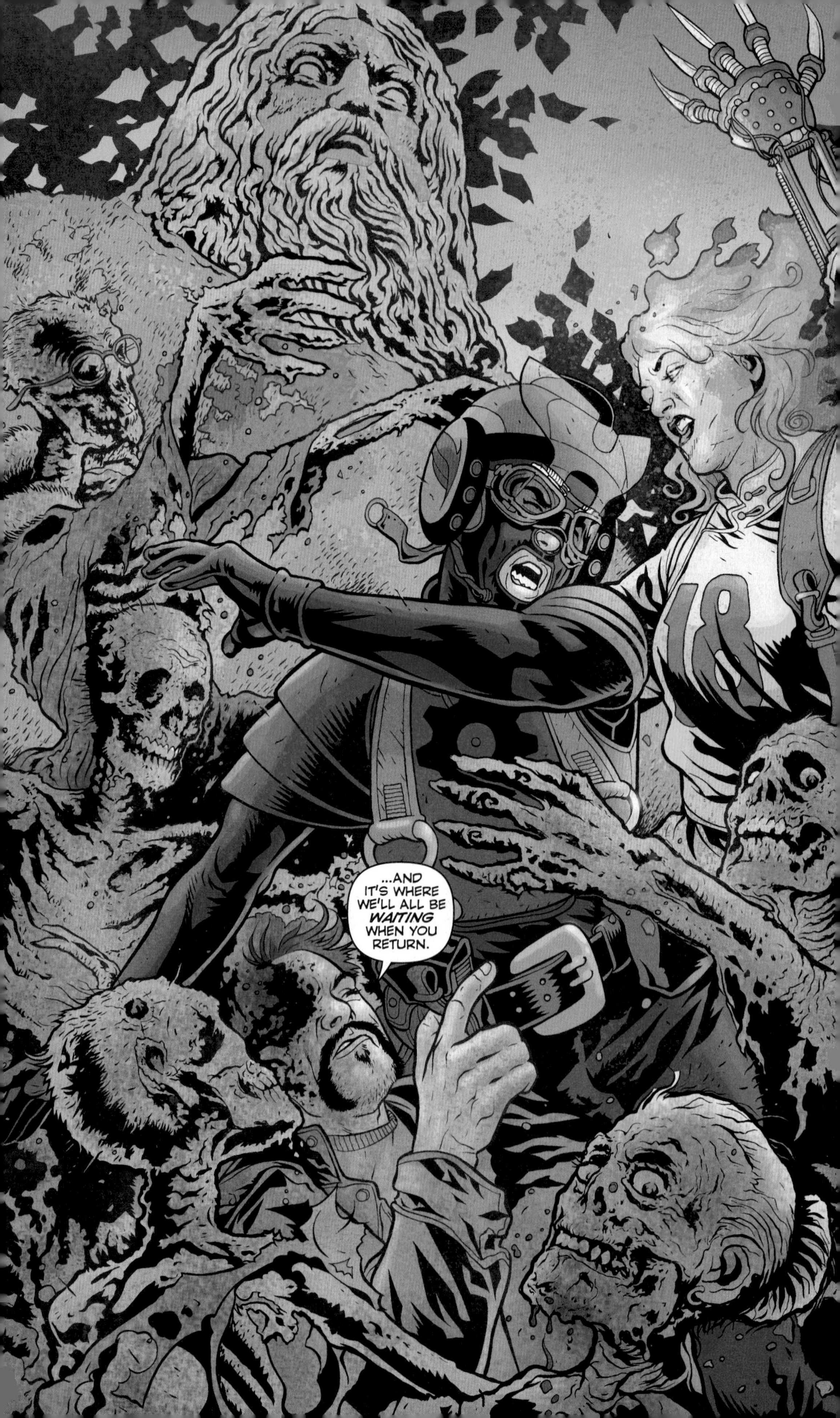
...AND IT'S WHERE WE'LL ALL BE *WAITING* WHEN YOU RETURN.

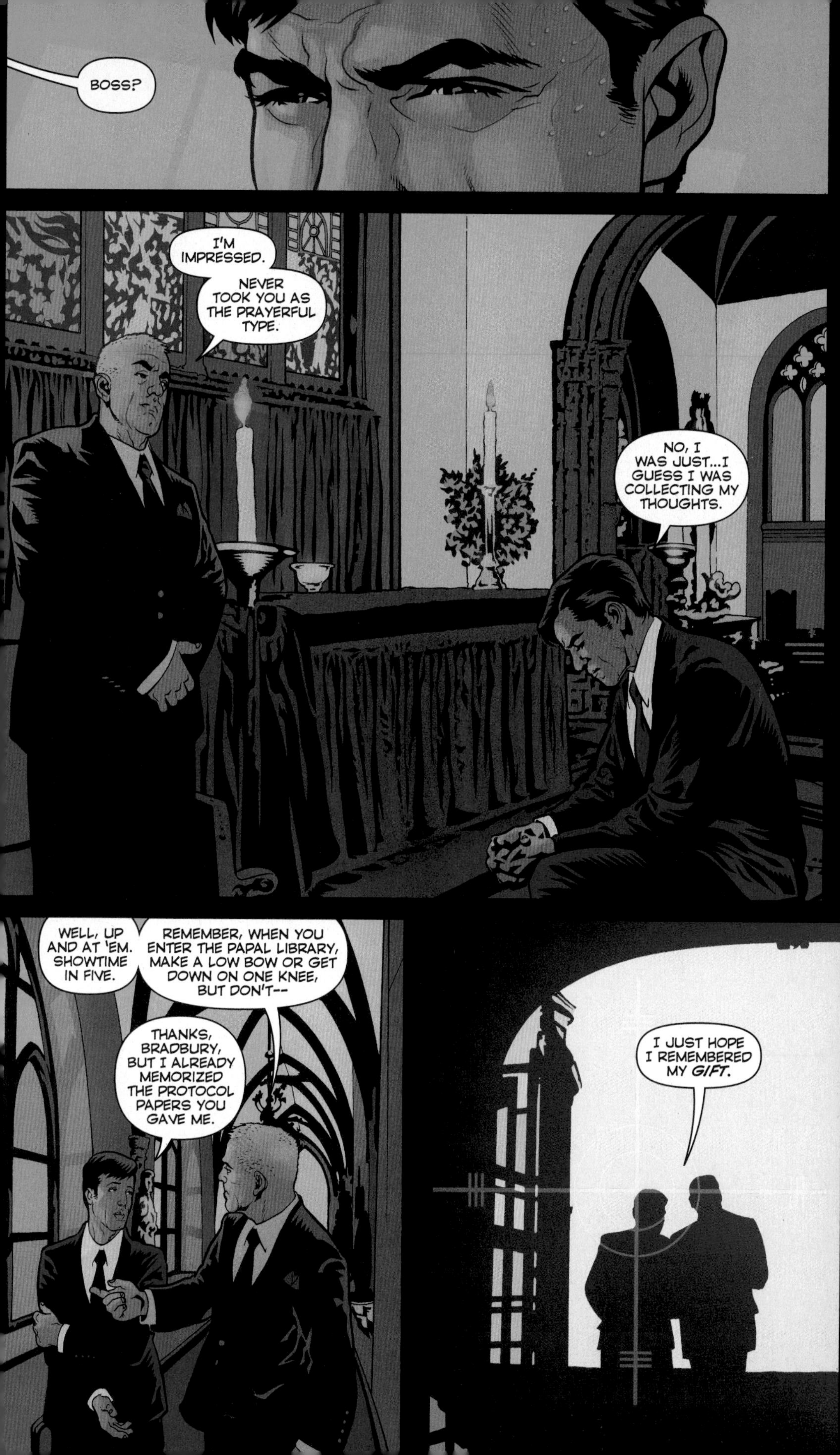
BOSS?
I'M IMPRESSED.
NEVER TOOK YOU AS THE PRAYERFUL TYPE.
NO, I WAS JUST...I GUESS I WAS COLLECTING MY THOUGHTS.
WELL, UP AND AT 'EM. SHOWTIME IN FIVE.
REMEMBER, WHEN YOU ENTER THE PAPAL LIBRARY, MAKE A LOW BOW OR GET DOWN ON ONE KNEE, BUT DON'T--
THANKS, BRADBURY, BUT I ALREADY MEMORIZED THE PROTOCOL PAPERS YOU GAVE ME.
I JUST HOPE I REMEMBERED MY *GIFT*.

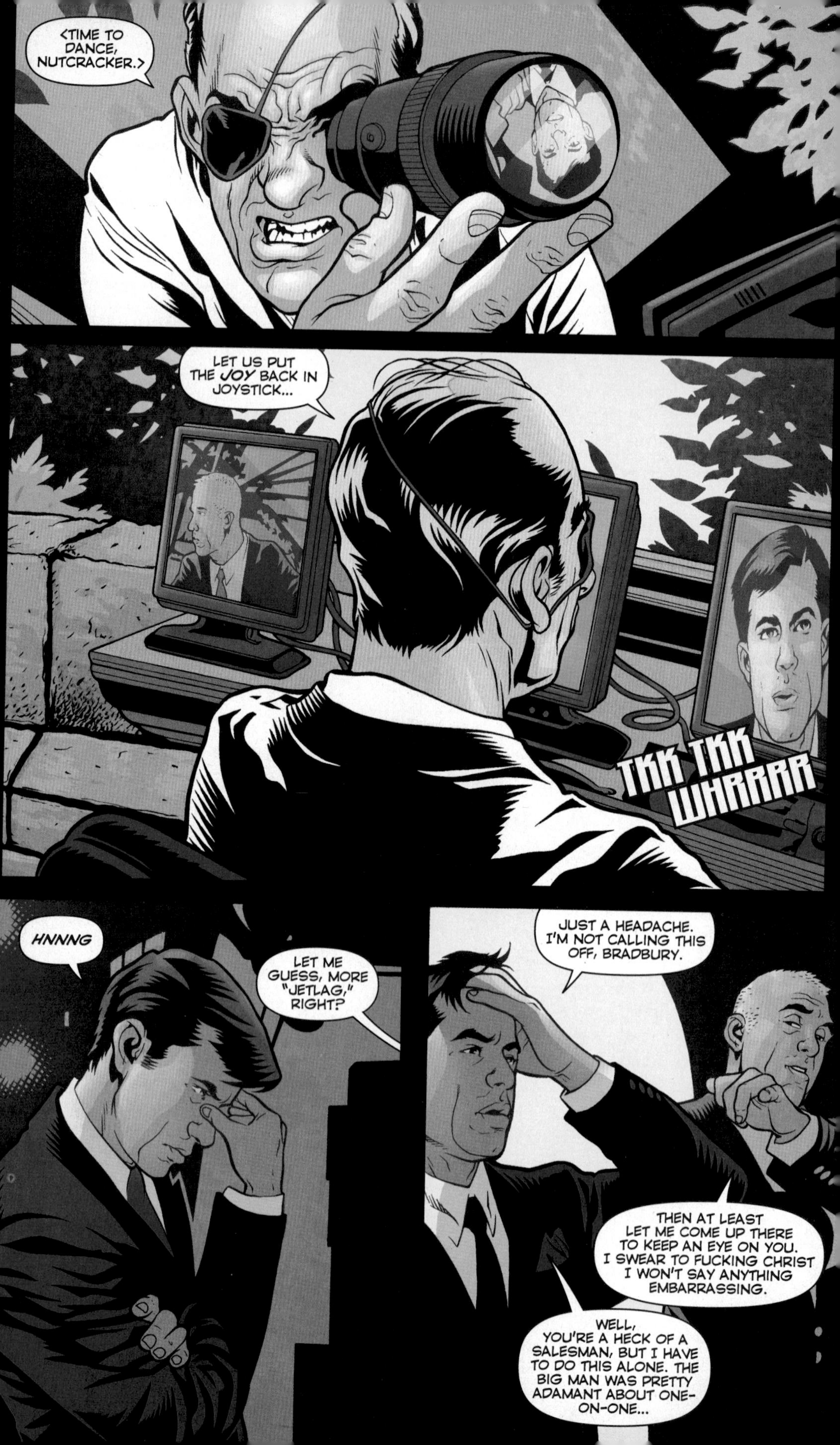
<TIME TO DANCE, NUTCRACKER.>
LET US PUT THE JOY BACK IN JOYSTICK...
TKK TKK WHRRRR
HNNNG
LET ME GUESS, MORE "JETLAG," RIGHT?
JUST A HEADACHE. I'M NOT CALLING THIS OFF, BRADBURY.
THEN AT LEAST LET ME COME UP THERE TO KEEP AN EYE ON YOU. I SWEAR TO FUCKING CHRIST I WON'T SAY ANYTHING EMBARRASSING.
WELL, YOU'RE A HECK OF A SALESMAN, BUT I HAVE TO DO THIS ALONE. THE BIG MAN WAS PRETTY ADAMANT ABOUT ONE-ON-ONE...

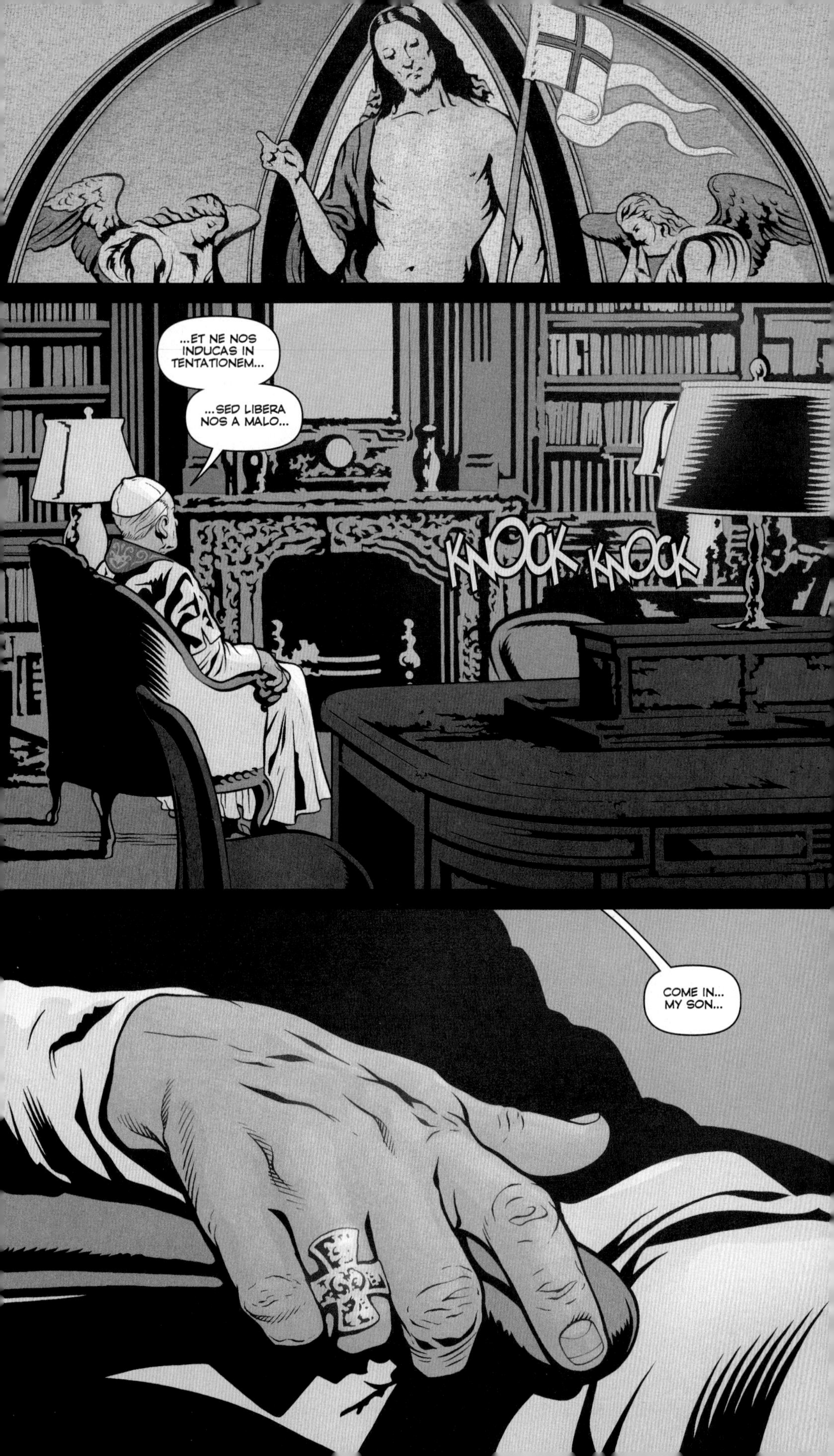
...ET NE NOS INDUCAS IN TENTATIONEM...
...SED LIBERA NOS A MALO...
KNOCK KNOCK
COME IN... MY SON...

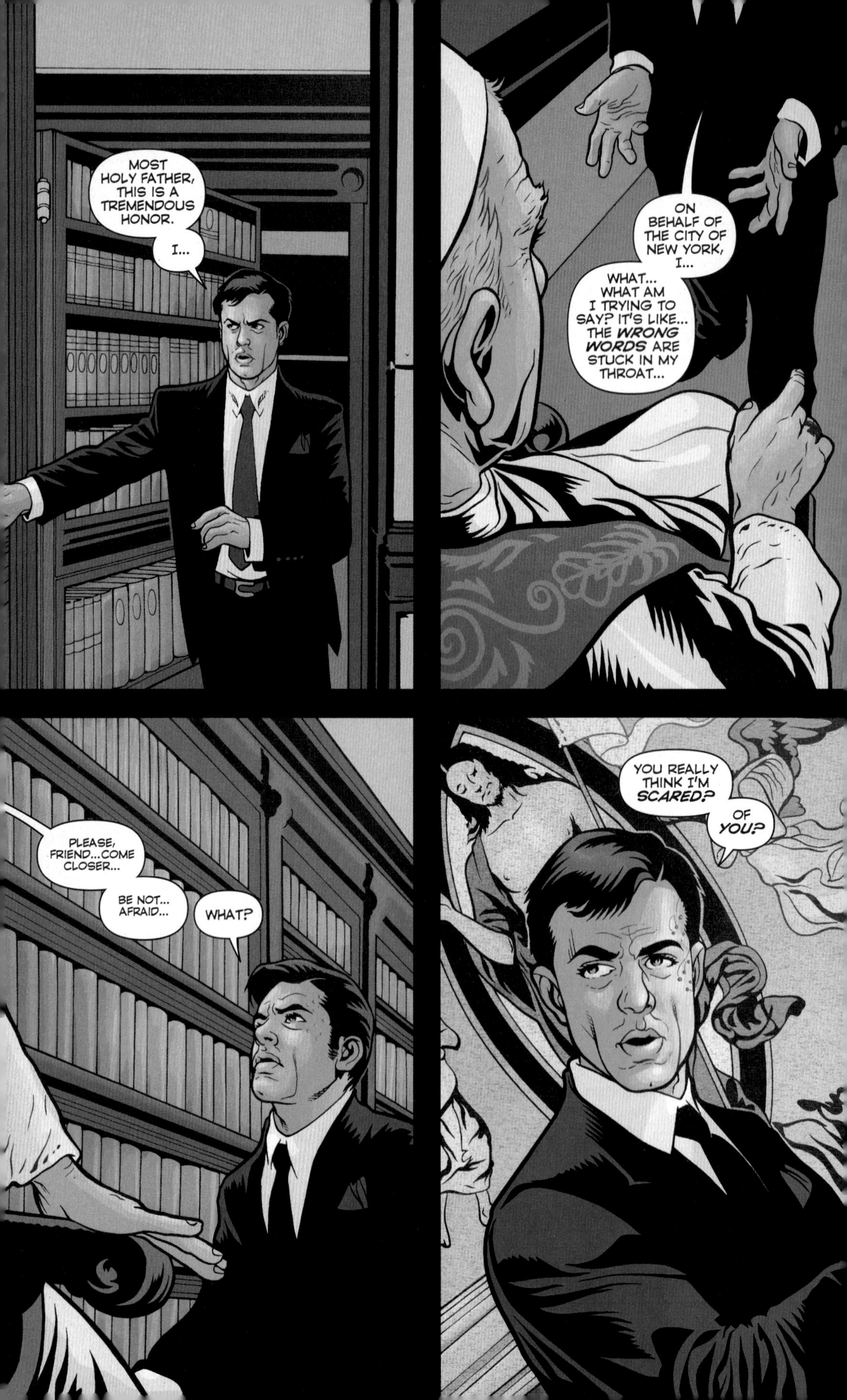
MOST HOLY FATHER, THIS IS A TREMENDOUS HONOR.
I...
ON BEHALF OF THE CITY OF NEW YORK, I...
WHAT... WHAT AM I TRYING TO SAY? IT'S LIKE... THE WRONG WORDS ARE STUCK IN MY THROAT...
PLEASE, FRIEND...COME CLOSER...
BE NOT... AFRAID...
WHAT?
YOU REALLY THINK I'M SCARED?
OF YOU?

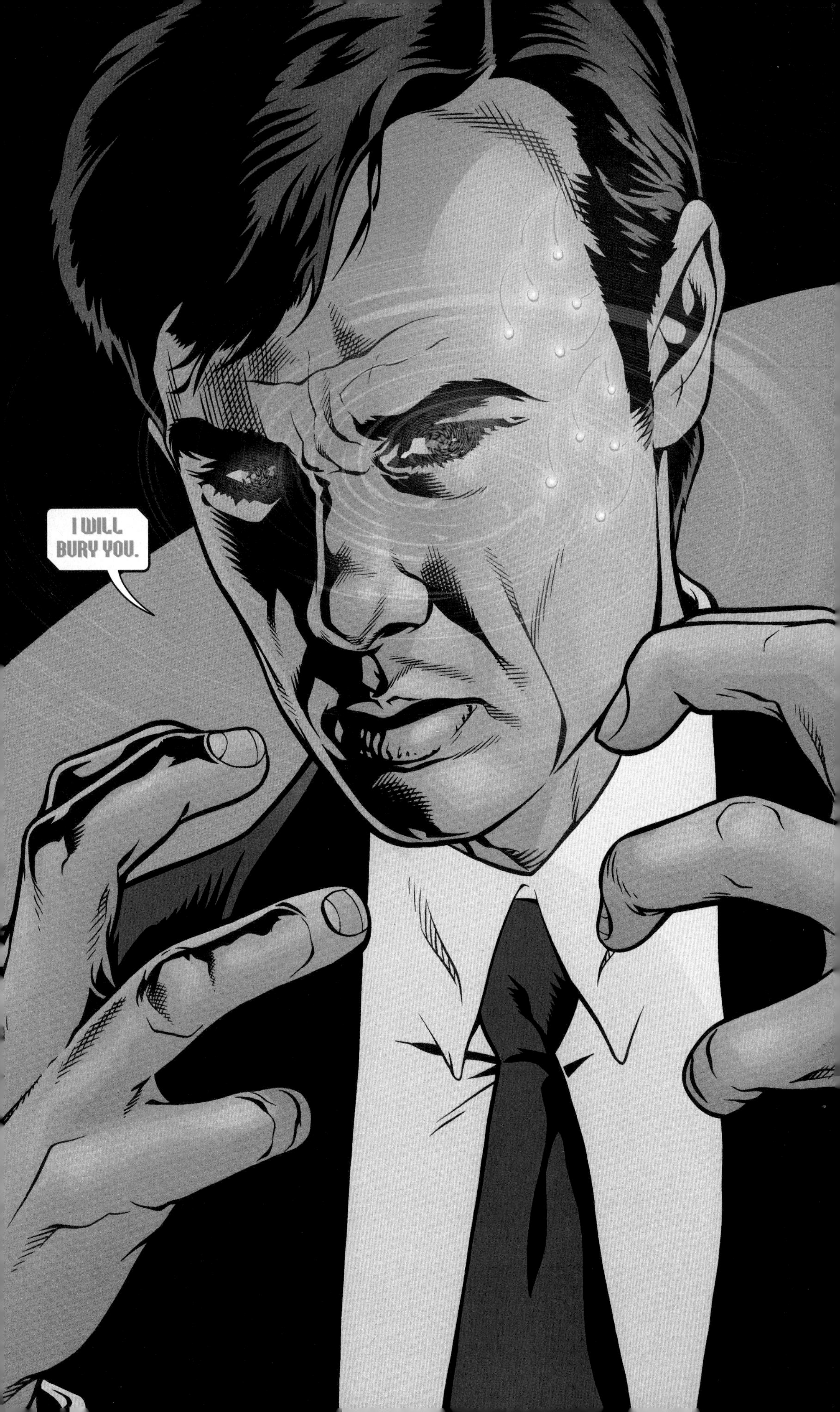
I WILL BURY YOU.

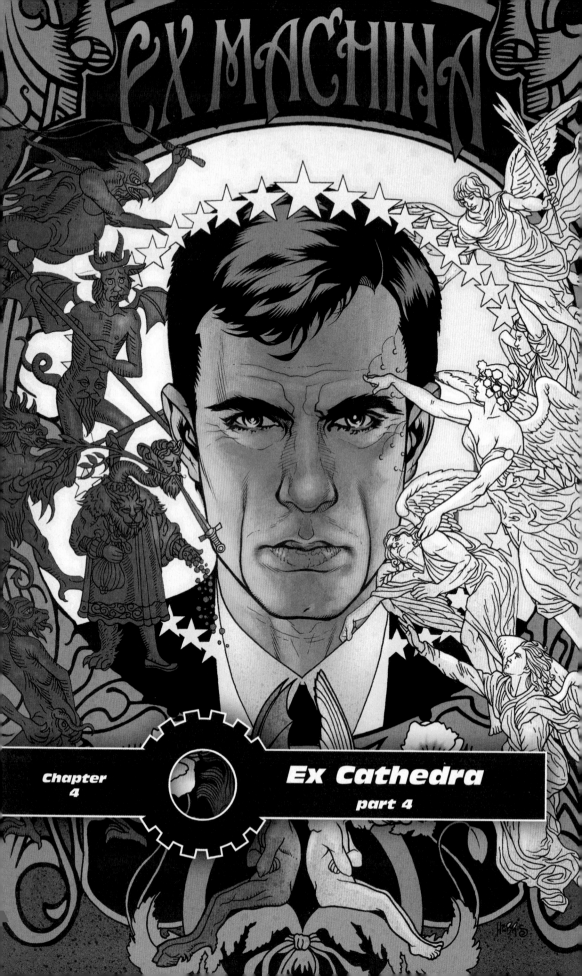

EX MACHINA

Ex Cathedra

part 4

Chapter 4

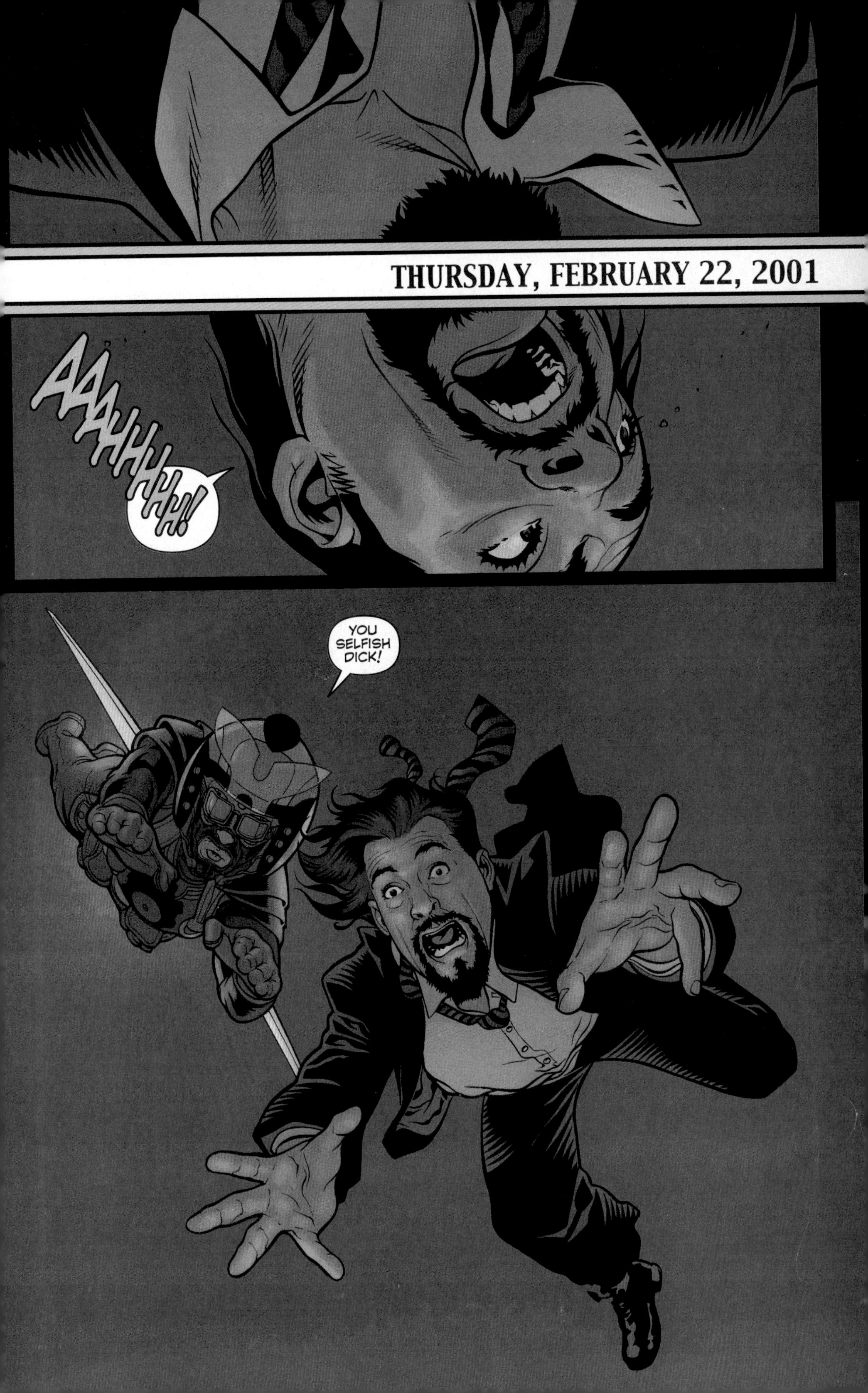
THURSDAY, FEBRUARY 22, 2001
AAAHHHHH!
YOU SELFISH DICK!

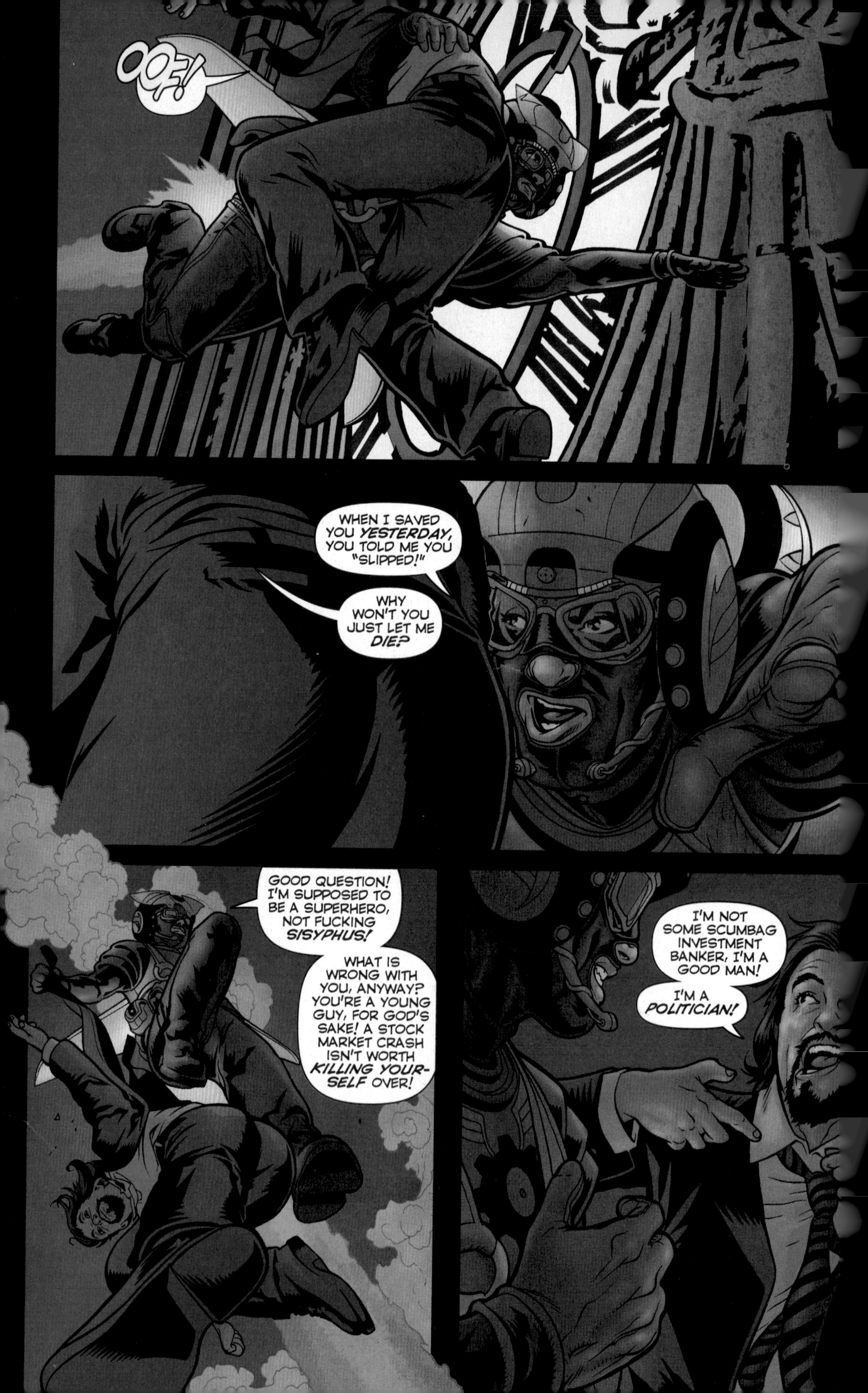
OOF!
WHEN I SAVED YOU YESTERDAY, YOU TOLD ME YOU "SLIPPED!"
WHY WON'T YOU JUST LET ME DIE?
GOOD QUESTION! I'M SUPPOSED TO BE A SUPERHERO, NOT FUCKING SISYPHUS!
WHAT IS WRONG WITH YOU, ANYWAY? YOU'RE A YOUNG GUY, FOR GOD'S SAKE! A STOCK MARKET CRASH ISN'T WORTH KILLING YOURSELF OVER!
I'M NOT SOME SCUMBAG INVESTMENT BANKER, I'M A GOOD MAN!
I'M A POLITICIAN!

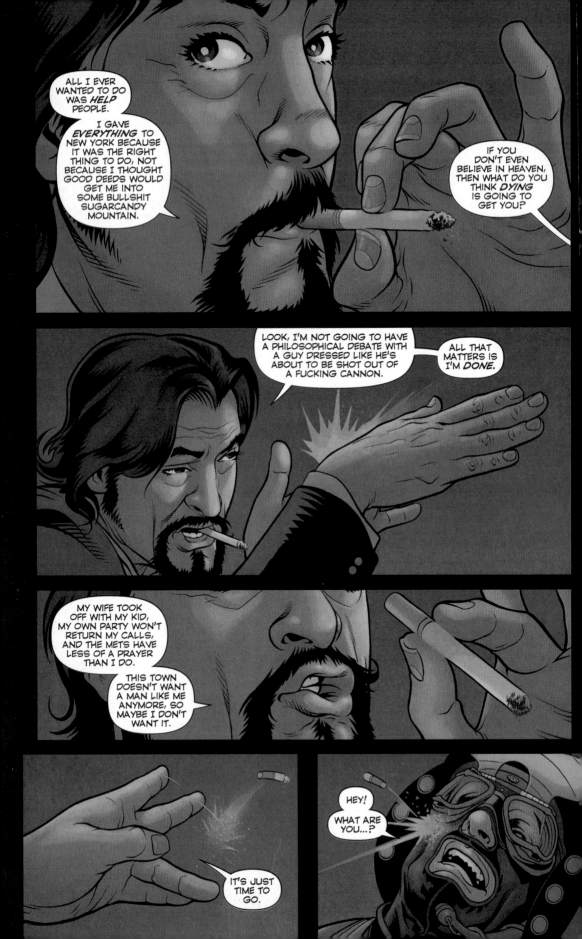

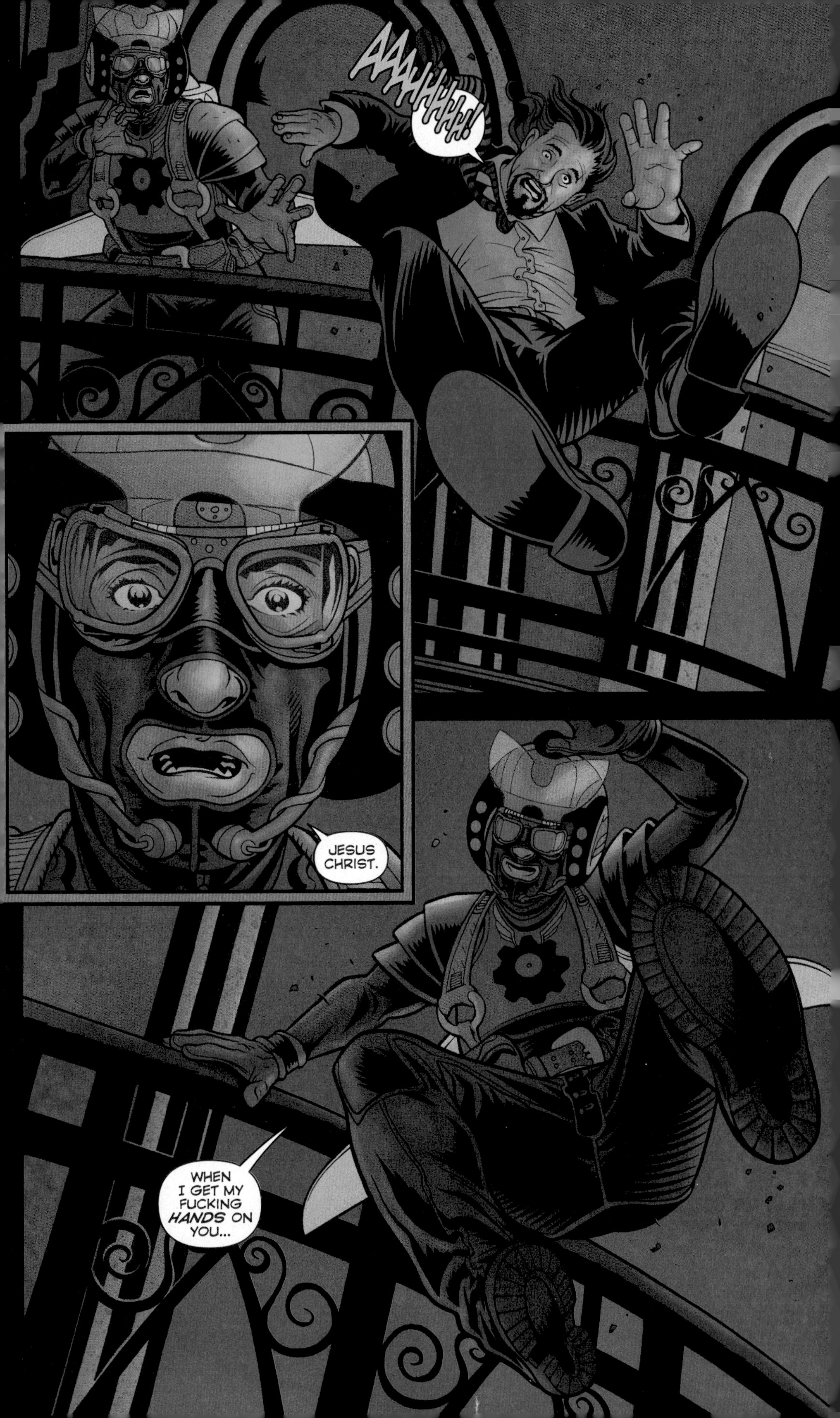
AAAHHHH!
JESUS CHRIST.
WHEN I GET MY FUCKING *HANDS* ON YOU...

MONDAY, DECEMBER 15, 2003

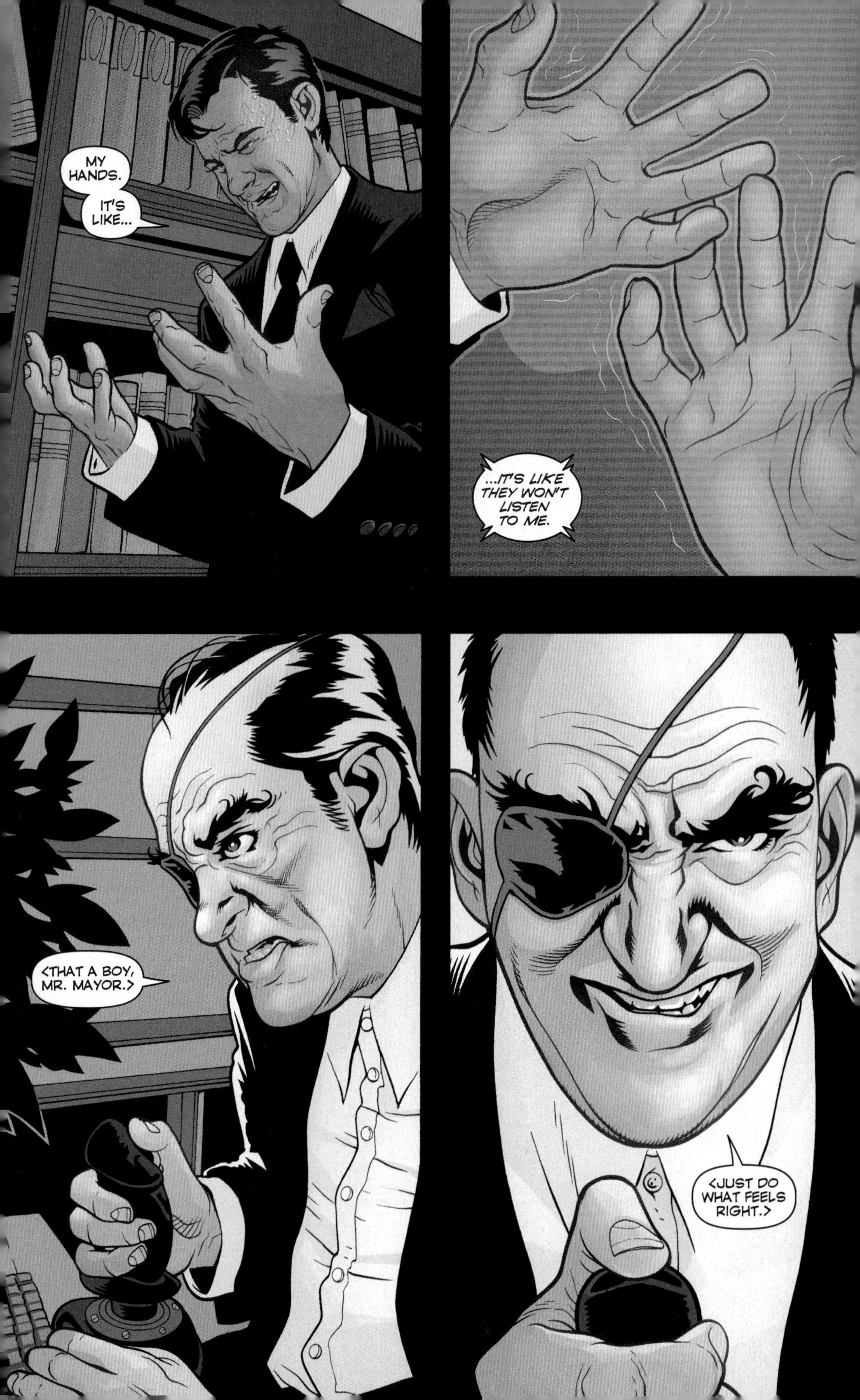
MY HANDS.
IT'S LIKE...
...IT'S LIKE THEY WON'T LISTEN TO ME.
<THAT A BOY, MR. MAYOR.>
<JUST DO WHAT FEELS RIGHT.>

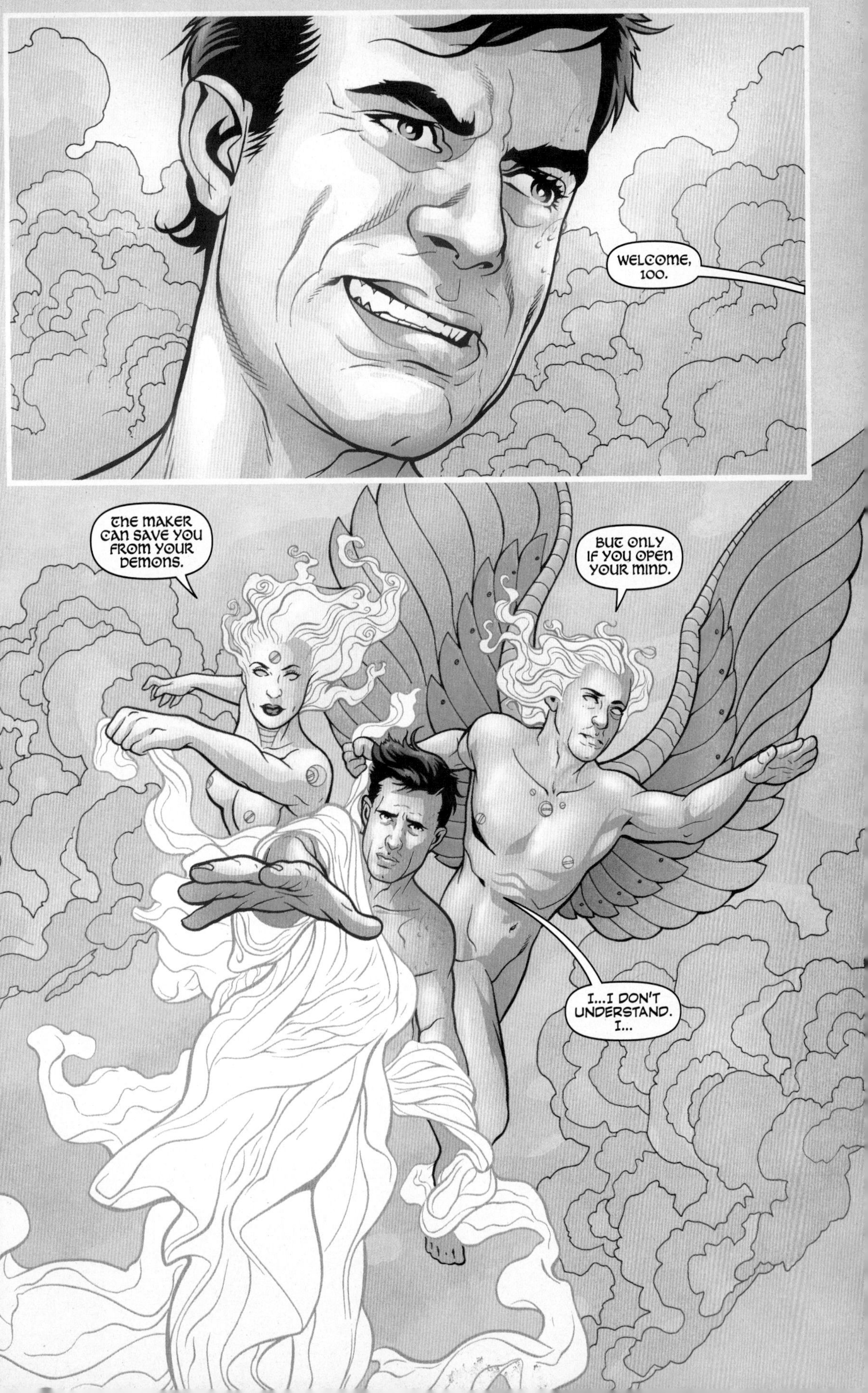
WELCOME, 100.
THE MAKER CAN SAVE YOU FROM YOUR DEMONS.
BUT ONLY IF YOU OPEN YOUR MIND.
I...I DON'T UNDERSTAND. I...

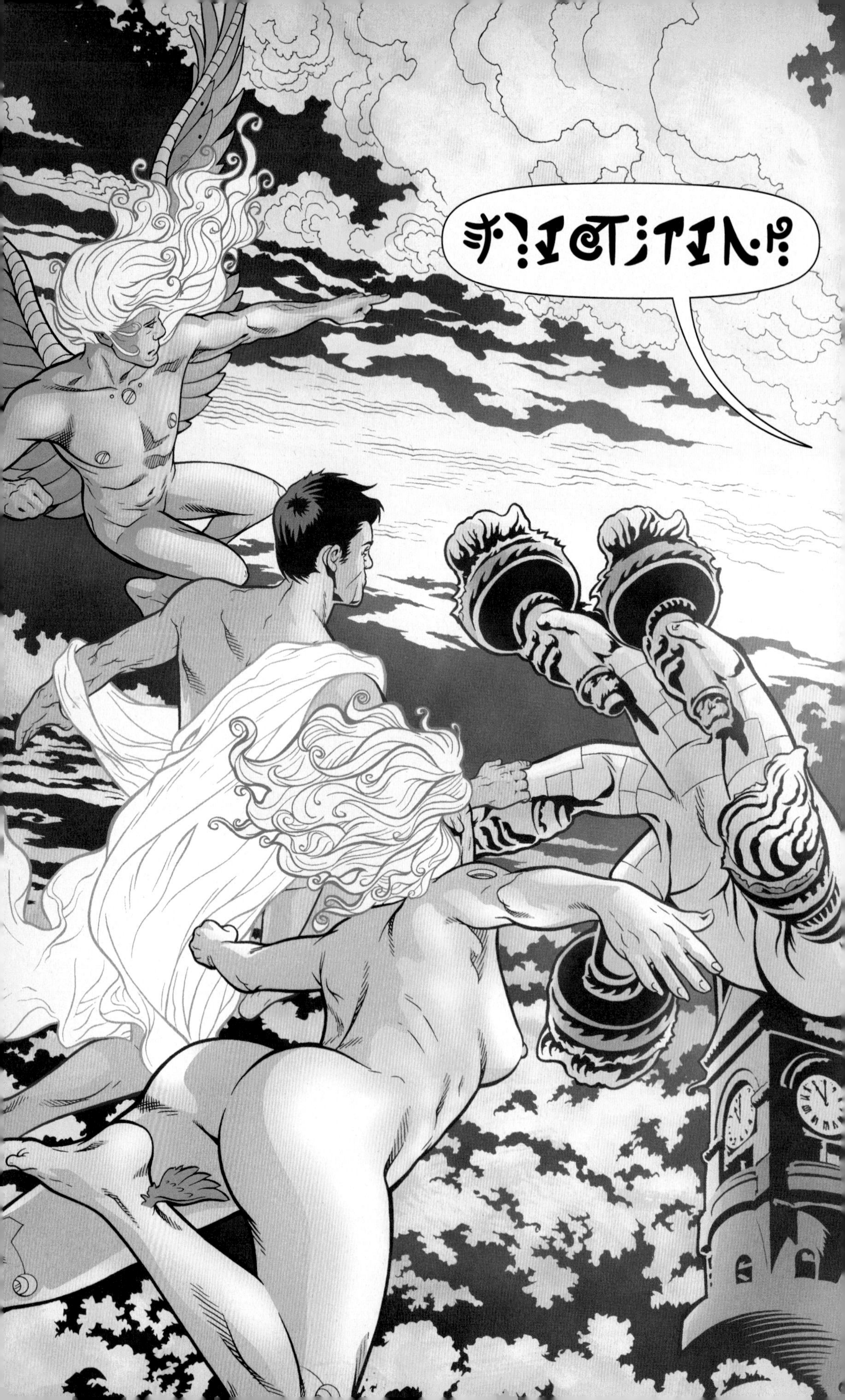

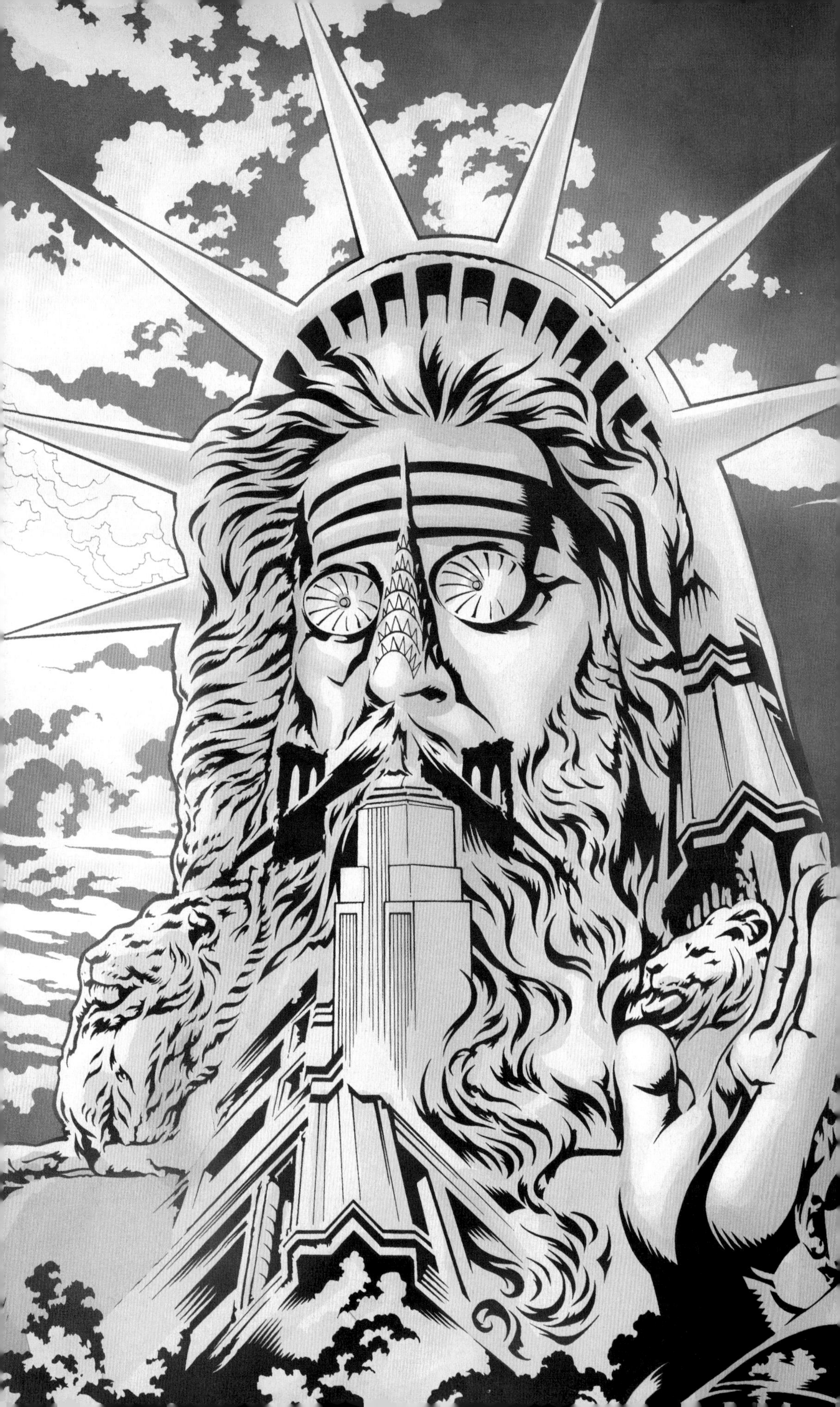

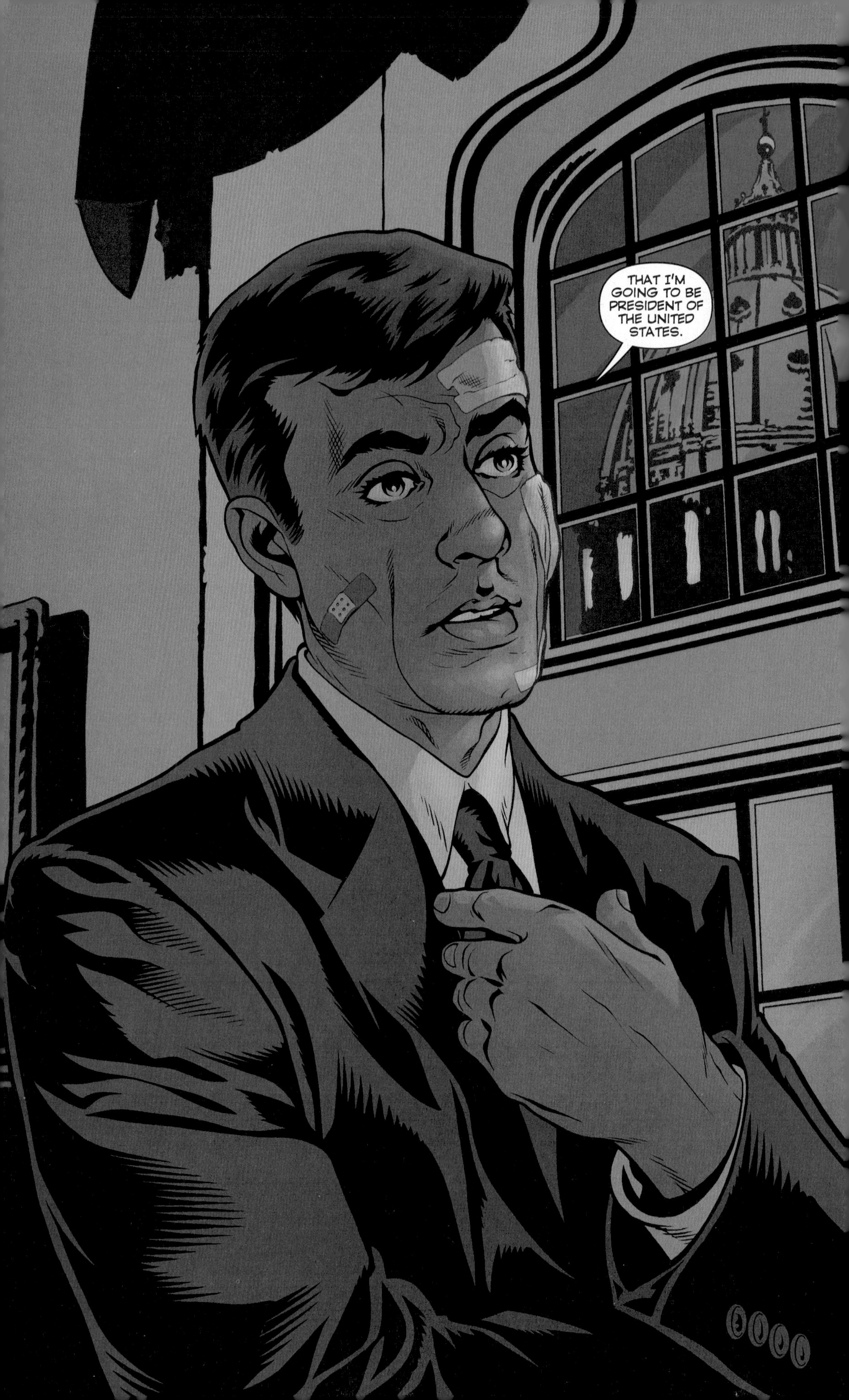
THAT I'M GOING TO BE PRESIDENT OF THE UNITED STATES.

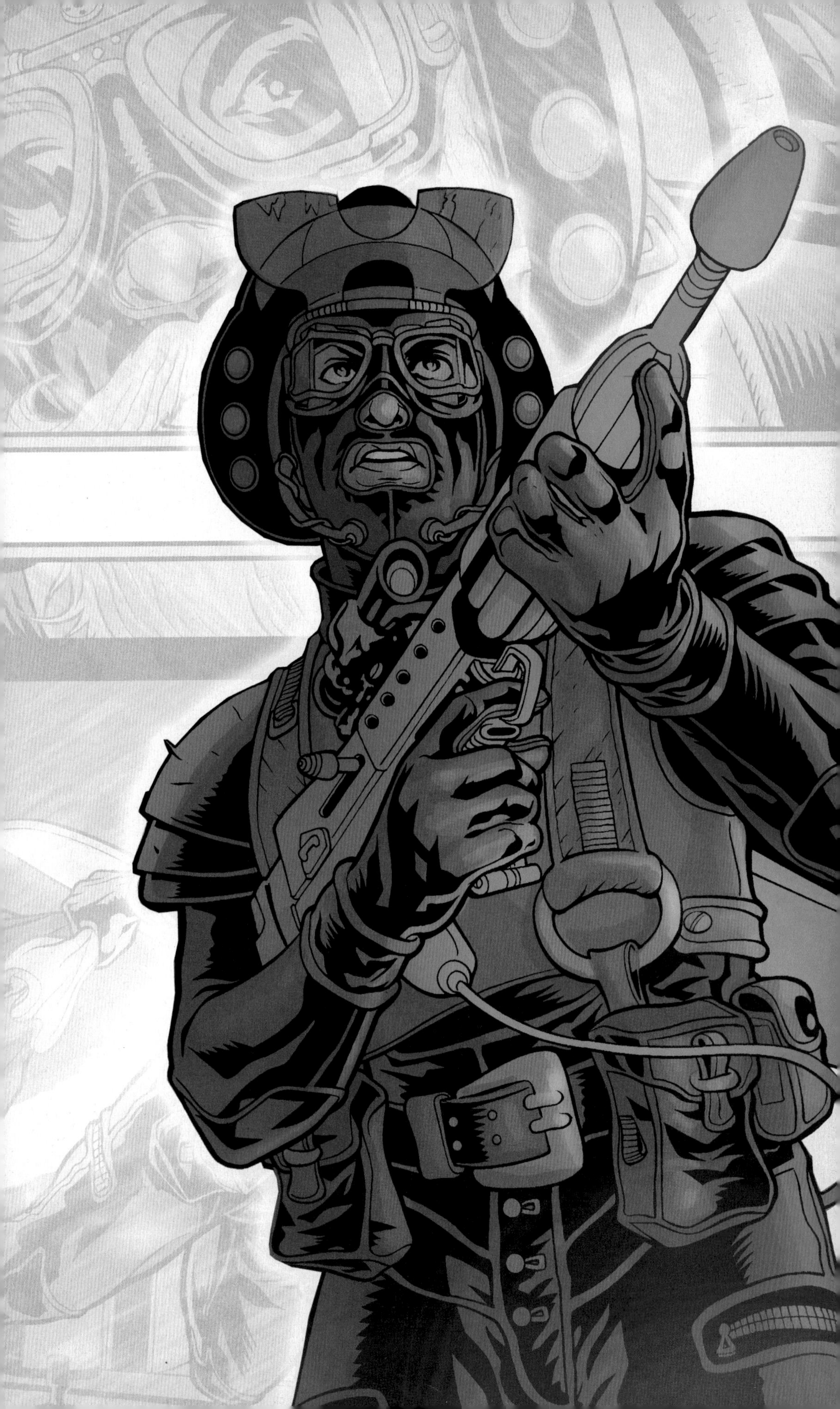

Chapter 5 World's Finest

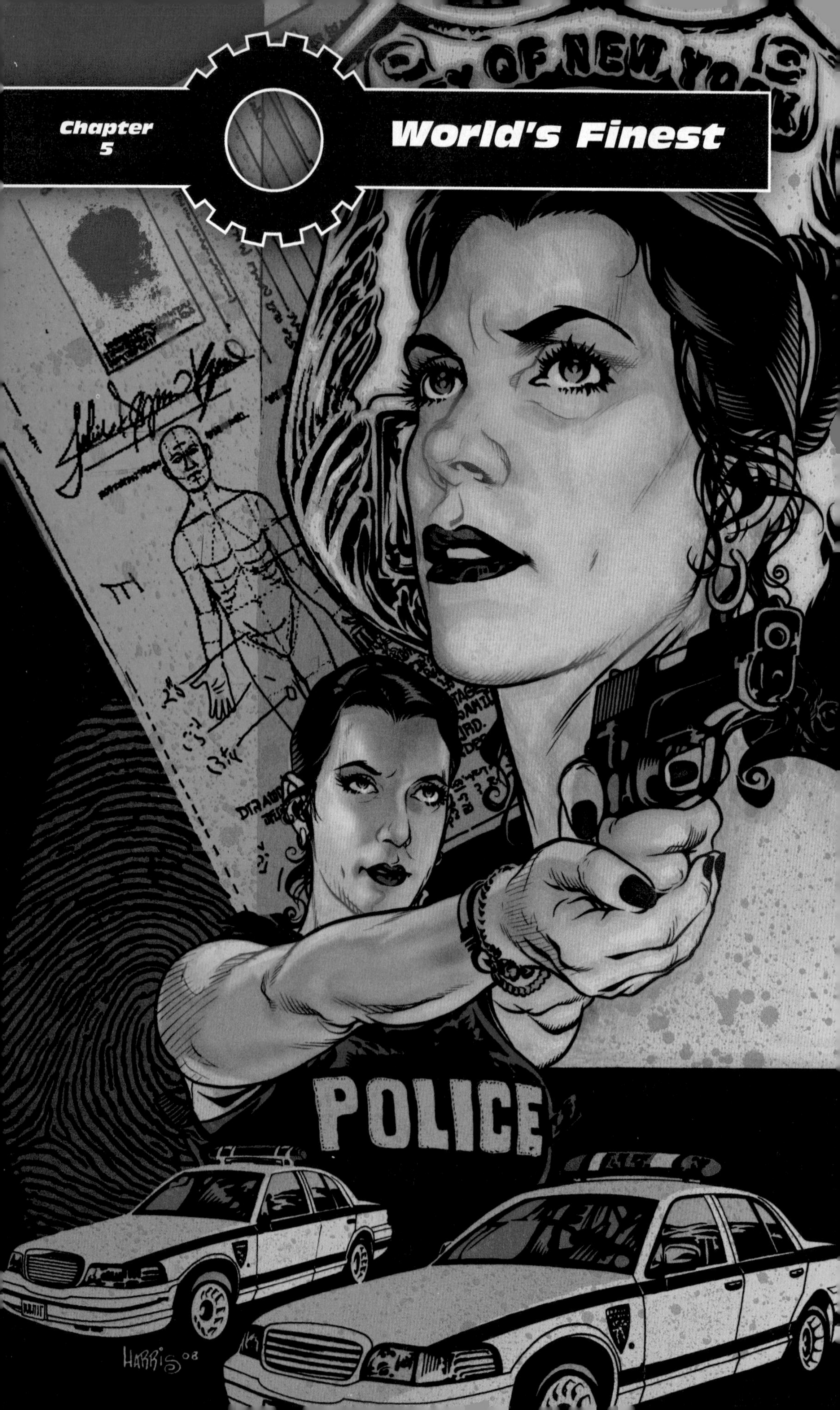
OF NEW YORK
POLICE
HARRIS 08

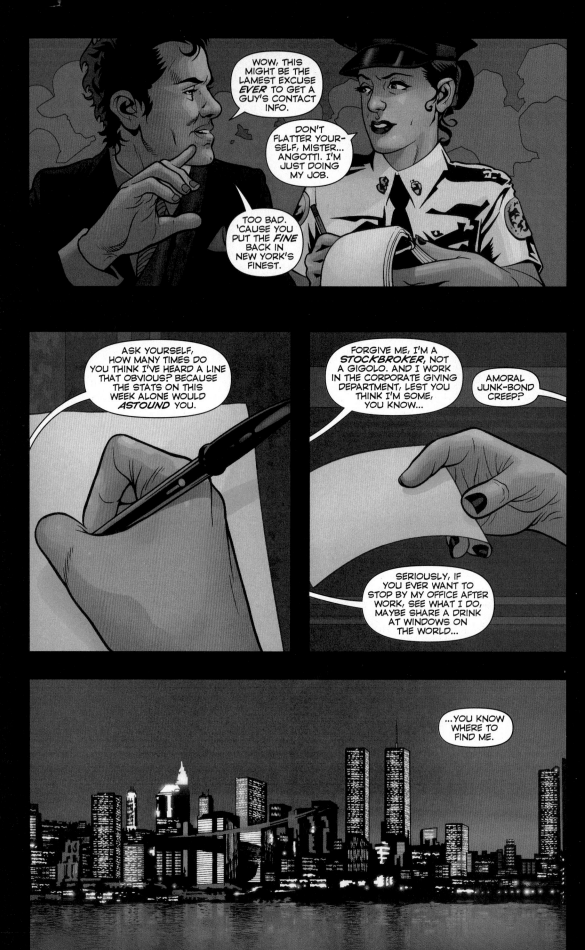

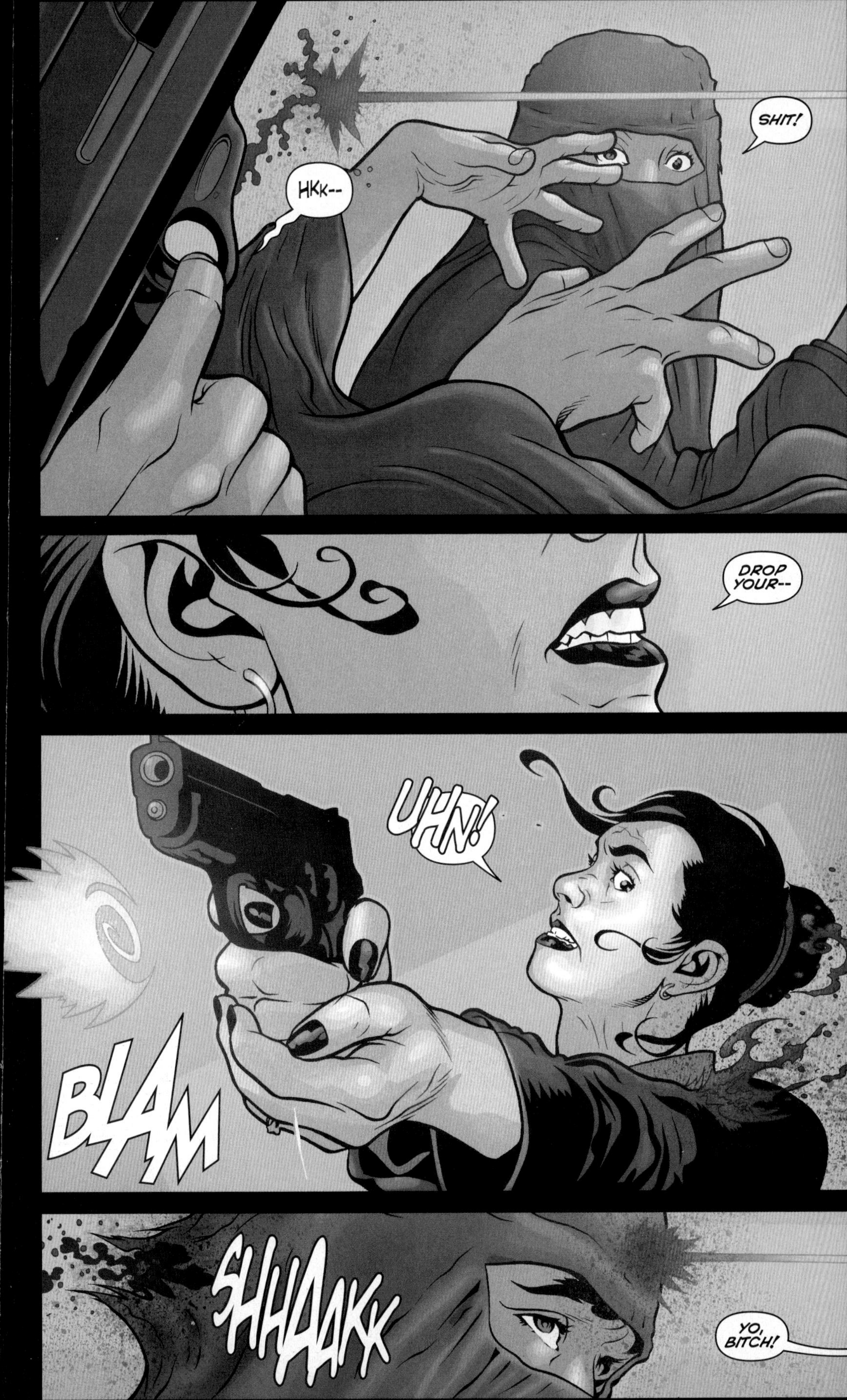
SHIT!
HKK--
DROP YOUR--
UHN!
BLAM
SHHAAKK
YO, BITCH!

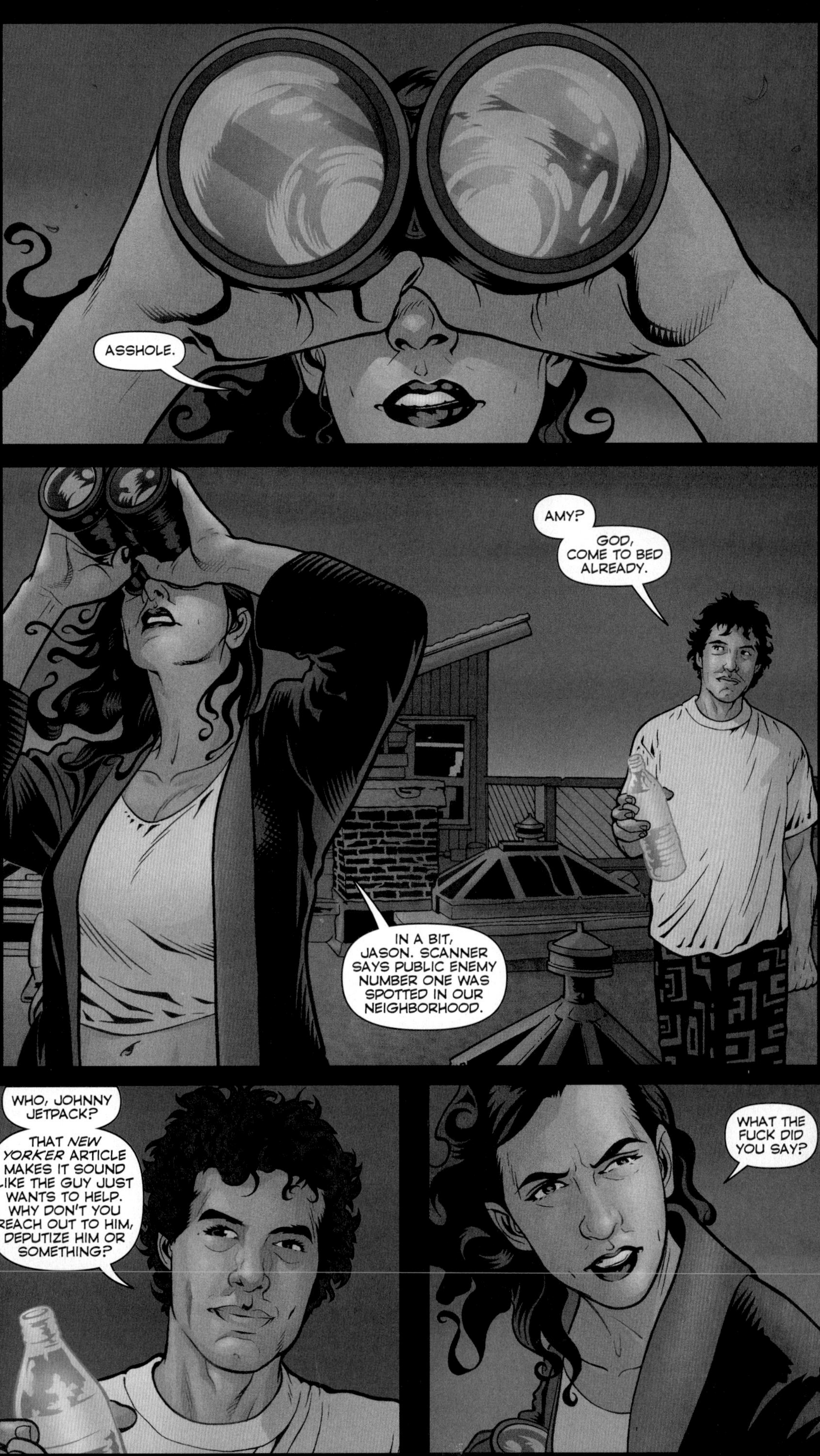
ASSHOLE.
AMY?
GOD, COME TO BED ALREADY.
IN A BIT, JASON. SCANNER SAYS PUBLIC ENEMY NUMBER ONE WAS SPOTTED IN OUR NEIGHBORHOOD.
WHO, JOHNNY JETPACK?
THAT *NEW YORKER* ARTICLE MAKES IT SOUND LIKE THE GUY JUST WANTS TO HELP. WHY DON'T YOU REACH OUT TO HIM, DEPUTIZE HIM OR SOMETHING?
WHAT THE FUCK DID YOU SAY?

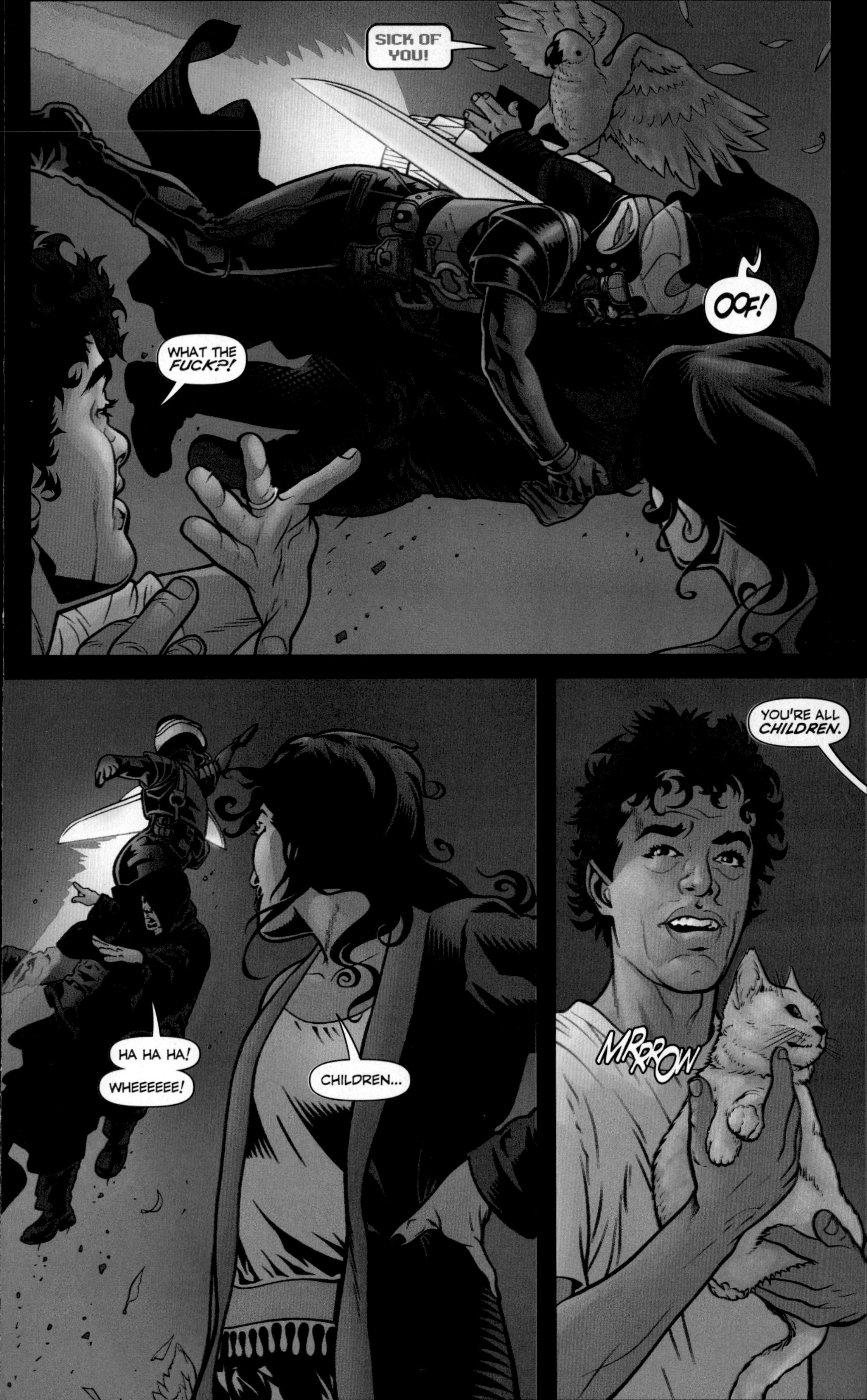
SICK OF YOU!
WHAT THE FUCK?!
OOF!
HA HA HA!
WHEEEEEE!
CHILDREN...
YOU'RE ALL CHILDREN.
MRRROW

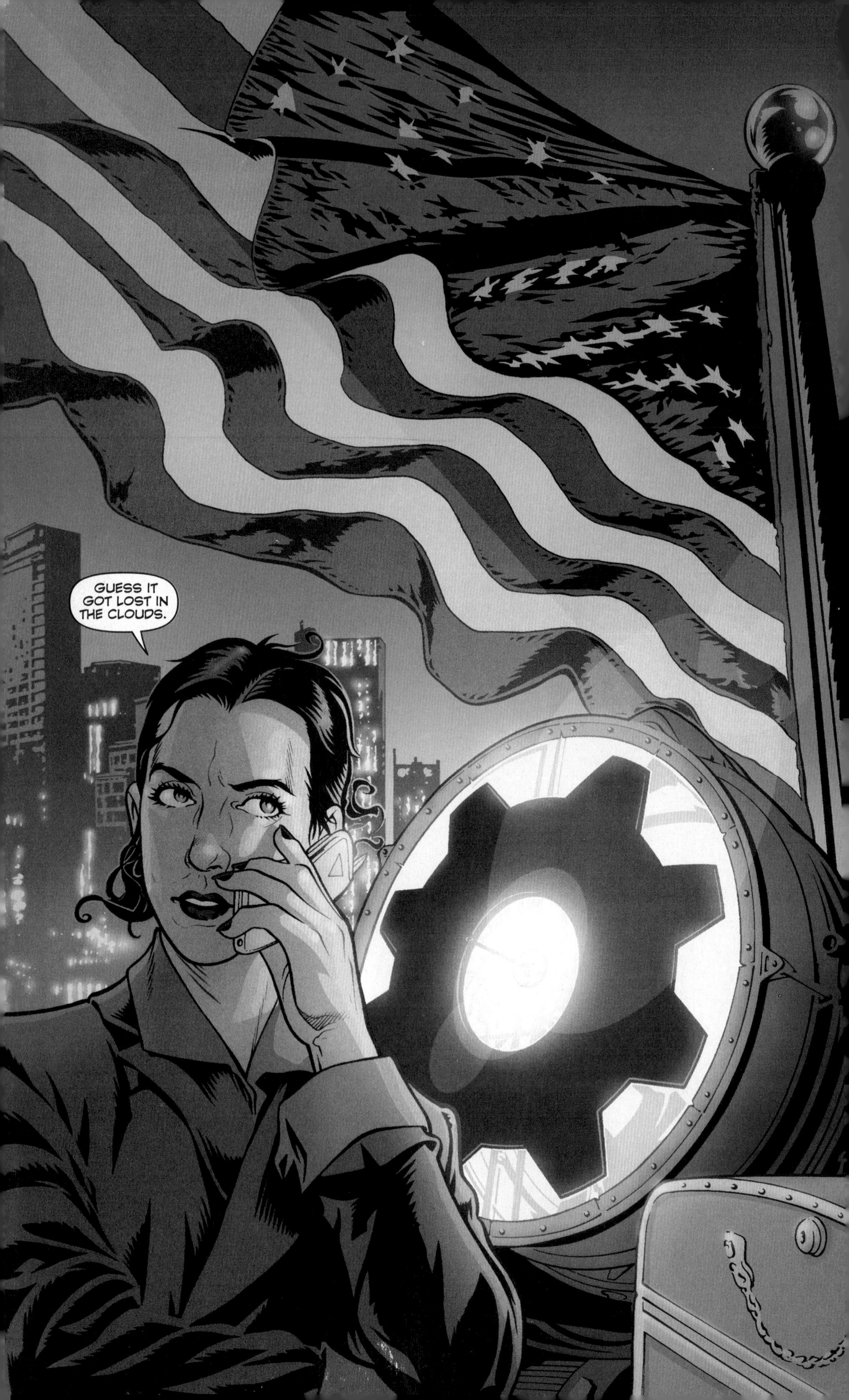
GUESS IT GOT LOST IN THE CLOUDS.

Look for this oversized hardcover!

EX MACHINA

The Deluxe Edition

After an accident left him with the ability to talk to machines, Mitchell Hundred became "the Great Machine" and fought crime, not always successfully. Then he retired from masked crimefighting and ran for Mayor of New York City...and won by a landslide. He might have been a second rate superhero—but now he's one hell of a Mayor.

"ONE OF THE 10 BEST FICTION NOVELS OF THE YEAR!"
-Entertainment Weekly
BRIAN K. VAUGHAN
TONY HARRIS
EX MACHINA
THE DELUXE EDITION
INTRODUCTION BY
BRAD MELTZER

The Deluxe Edition collects the first 11 issues, and features an introduction by best-selling writer Brad Meltzer, plus the original series proposal. Or check out the regular trade paperbacks:

Book 1: The First Hundred Days
Book 2: Tag
Book 3: Fact v. Fiction
Book 4: March to War
Book 5: Smoke Smoke
Book 6: Power Down

More books by these creators:

PRIDE OF BAGHDAD

BRIAN K. VAUGHAN
NIKO HENRICHON
PRIDE
of
baghdad
VERTIGO

Vaughan • Henrichon

STARMAN OMNIBUS

STARMAN
OMNIBUS
"The best-written superhero in comics..."
—Entertainment Weekly
JAMES ROBINSON TONY HARRIS WADE VON GRAWBADGER

Robinson • Harris

Y: THE LAST MAN

VERTIGO
BOOK 4
"Has steadily proved to be one of the best examples of its art form... Fascinating."
— The Chicago Tribune
"Complete and utter comic gold."
— Publishers Weekly (starred review)
Vaughan Guerra Parlov Marzán, Jr.
Y
THE LAST MAN
Safeword

Vaughan • Guerra
Various

SEARCH THE GRAPHIC NOVELS SECTION OF

www.WILDSTORM.com

FOR ART AND INFORMATION ON ALL OF OUR BOOKS!

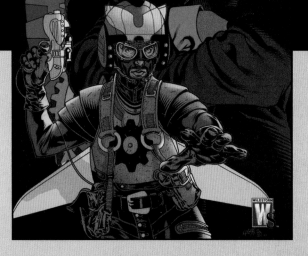

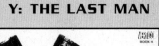

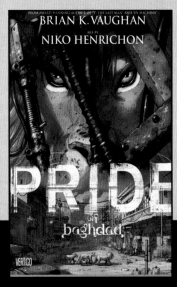

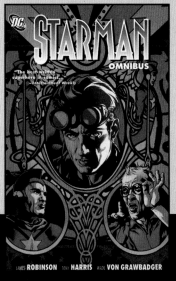

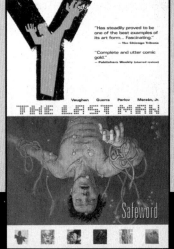

WILDSTORM: ARMAGEDDON

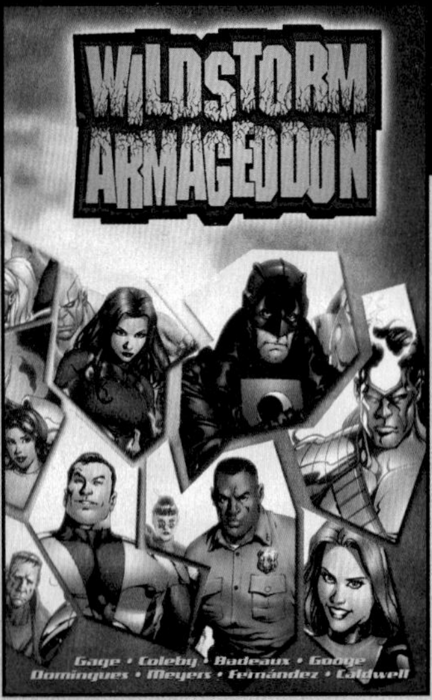
WILDSTORM ARMAGEDDON
Gage • Coleby • Badeaux • Googe
Domingues • Meyers • Fernández • Caldwell

GAGE • VARIOUS

WILDSTORM: REVELATIONS

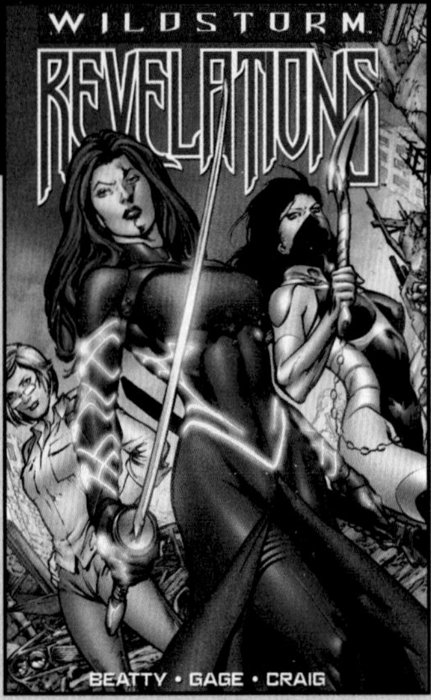
WILDSTORM
REVELATIONS
BEATTY • GAGE • CRAIG

BEATTY • GAGE
CRAIG

NUMBER OF THE BEAST

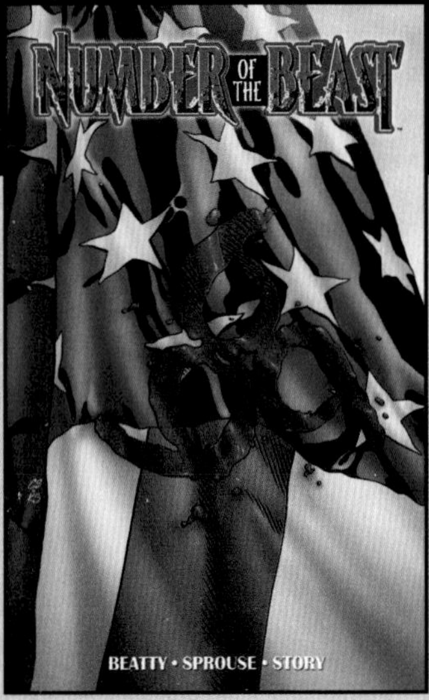
NUMBER OF THE BEAST
BEATTY • SPROUSE • STORY

BEATTY • SPROUSE
STORY • VARIOUS

MIDNIGHTER
BOOKS 1 & 2

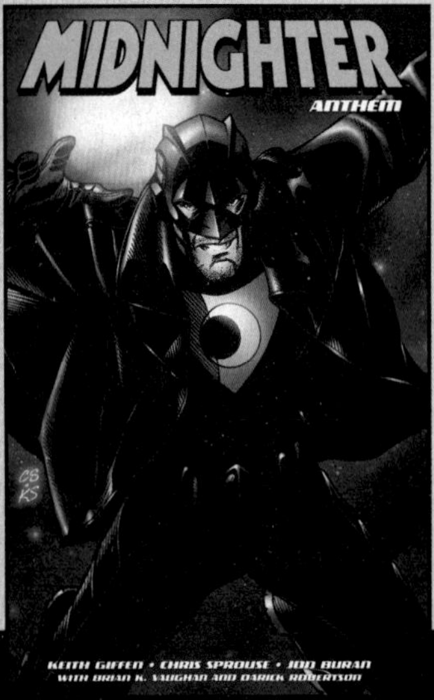
MIDNIGHTER
ANTHEM
KEITH GIFFEN • CHRIS SPROUSE • JON BURAN
WITH BRIAN K. VAUGHAN AND DARICK ROBERTSON

VARIOUS WRITERS & ARTISTS

STORMWATCH: PHD
BOOKS 1 & 2

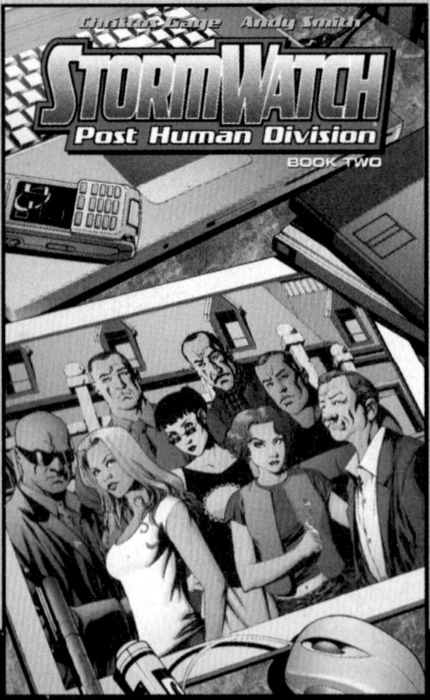
Christos Gage
Andy Smith
STORMWATCH
Post Human Division
BOOK TWO

GAGE • MAHNKE
SMITH

WELCOME TO TRANQUILITY
BOOKS 1 & 2

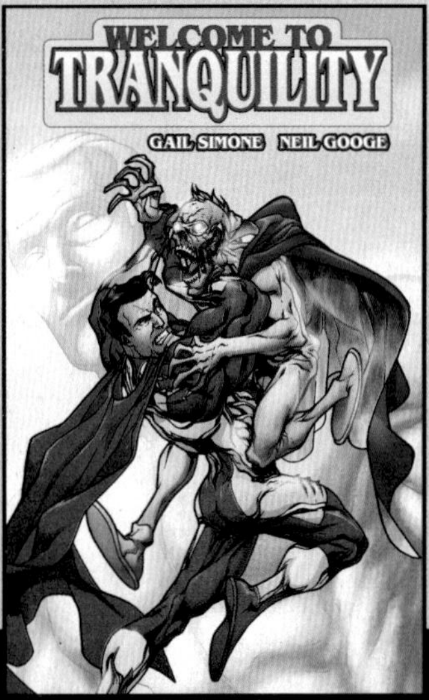
WELCOME TO TRANQUILITY
GAIL SIMONE
NEIL GOOGE

SIMONE • GOOGE

TO FIND MORE COLLECTED EDITIONS AND MONTHLY COMIC BOOKS FROM WILDSTORM AND DC COMICS

CALL 1-888-COMIC BOOK

FOR THE NEAREST COMICS SHOP OR GO TO YOUR LOCAL BOOK STORE